Praise for *The Lean Tech Manifesto*

If you are adopting Agile across your organization, but sense that something vital may be missing from your approach, this is an important book for you. Within these pages you will find a wealth of ideas that may lead you to discover solutions for *your* particular challenges, in pursuit of a "learning organization" that will prepare you to skillfully meet the challenges of an uncertain future.

—**Steve Bell**, two-time Shingo Research Award recipient, author of *Lean IT* and *Run Grow Transform*

If Lean thinking alone were enough, the most valuable car company in the world would still be Toyota. But it isn't. This is the book you need, combining the experience of mastering Agile with Lean Thinking. With this book you can prevent hierarchical slowdown and keep people at the center as you scale up and automate.

—**Joe Justice**, author of *Scrum Master*, creator of eXtreme Manufacturing, founder of Wikispeed, lecturer on #JoeDX, Tesla alum

After more than twenty years, it was clear that the Agile Manifesto needed Kaizen. This book is doing exactly that, based on the rare experience of a tech company that has combined agility with the genuine Toyota Production System (Lean), implemented thoroughly with some of the best sensei. I highly recommend it to all those who want to deliver more and more value to their customers. And there should not be any others.

—**Dr. Pierre Masai**, Lean coach, former CIO of Toyota Motor Europe, and Senior Advisor to Toyota Systems Corporation in Japan

Scaling your business while remaining agile can feel like an impossible task, but fear not! Fabrice and Benoît have developed a practical playbook that is based on their deep experience, providing you with the tools you need to continue to reap the benefits of Lean as your business grows.

—**Colin Bryar**, coauthor of *Working Backwards* and former VP at Amazon

The Lean Tech

Manifesto

Learn the secrets
of tech leaders
to grasp the full
benefits of
Agile at scale

Fabrice Bernhard and
Benoît Charles-Lavauzelle

Mc
Graw
Hill

1 2 3 4 5 6 7 8 9   LCR   29 28 27 26 25 24

ISBN   978-1-260-45902-9
MHID   1-260-45902-0

e-ISBN   978-1-260-45903-6
e-MHID   1-260-45903-9

This publication is designed to provide accurate and authoritative information in regard to the subject matter covered. It is sold with the understanding that neither the author nor the publisher is engaged in rendering legal, accounting, securities trading, or other professional services. If legal advice or other expert assistance is required, the services of a competent professional person should be sought.

—From a Declaration of Principles Jointly Adopted
by a Committee of the American Bar Association
and a Committee of Publishers and Associations

McGraw Hill books are available at special quantity discounts to use as premiums and sales promotions or for use in corporate training programs. To contact a representative, please visit the Contact Us pages at www.mhprofessional.com.

McGraw Hill is committed to making our products accessible to all learners. To learn more about the available support and accommodations we offer, please contact us at accessibility@mheducation.com. We also participate in the Access Text Network (www.accesstext.org), and ATN members may submit requests through ATN.

For all Theodoers,
your enthusiasm to always look
for better ways is a ceaseless source of motivation.

CONTENTS

PART FOUR
Produce Higher Quality with Right-First-Time

PART FIVE
Deliver Continuously with Just-in-Time

PART SIX
Continue Innovating by Building
a Learning Organization

PART SEVEN
Conclusion

FOREWORD

Business as usual, it is now clear, will not be enough to meet the existential challenges facing the world. If we are to keep up with the pace of change, we will need to develop creative new solutions and learn to scale them much more quickly. That is what this book is about. It tells the story of Theodo, a tech pioneer company at the heart of this struggle, designing new tech systems for startups and corporations. Over the past decade or so, Theodo has found new and more effective ways to work with one another and with clients and to scale their activities as the business grew from 10 to 700 people and generated revenues of $100 million.

Theodo achieved this by constantly challenging established best business practices—including Agile—and seeking new ones by testing what works in a tech business and what doesn't. It distills its lessons into the Lean Tech Manifesto, so others can learn from its experiences. The lessons it shares don't only apply to tech firms but are equally relevant to established businesses struggling to avoid the bureaucratic r ¡idities that slow them down as they grow.

A key source of inspiration for Theodo—and the antidote it has found to bureaucracy—has been Lean thinking and the set of values, principles, and practices behind Toyota's business system, which propelled Toyota to number one in the auto industry. Over 30 years ago, Western carmakers scrambled to respond to the discovery that Toyota could produce a car with zero defects with half the human effort and cost, a feat Toyota accomplished by developing the problem-solving skills of frontline teams to master their own work to achieve "right-first-time-on-time-every-time" and analyze the root causes of every interruption. Over time, they could then link upstream and downstream steps in a just-in-time flow from raw materials to finished goods, triggered by the pull of demand. The famous Toyota Production System turns out to be a learning system for the synchronization and continuous improvement of any organization, no matter how complex.

Less widely known was that Toyota also learned how to design a new car in half the time and with half the effort and cost, turning traditional "waterfall" project management into a continuous development system for successive product generations. Again, the team monitors progress and right-first-time and addresses problems immediately, so steps can be tightly synchronized. This system is led by a chief engineer, who captures information and feedback from customers, engineering, and production and decides what needs to change and what needs to stay the same for the next product generation, instead of changing everything at once.

This book also tells how these ideas had a profound influence on tech industry pioneers Steve Jobs and Jeff Bezos and led to many new software development practices of the Agile movement, like Extreme programming, Scrum, and devops. Critically, and this is perhaps its biggest contribution, it also describes how Agile practices can only be scaled by embedding them in a learning organization focused on developing capabilities through systematic learning by problem solving.

These different ways of working together also present new challenges for leaders, as authors Fabrice Bernhard and Benoît Charles-Lavauzelle have learned while creating and scaling up Theodo's own Lean system over the course of the past decade. The nature of decision-making, they realized, changes—from buying expertise to doing things for you, to hiring the right talent and developing internal capabilities. Direction is set by articulating the performance gaps to be closed and aligning the activities of teams around them. Finally, the development of teams' problem-solving capabilities to close those gaps happens thanks to the deployment of the most experienced associates as teachers and mentors.

This is an important book. It describes the business system that organizations around the world so desperately need, and it reminds us that when it comes to solving the complex and urgent problems of our time, human decision-making and teamwork are just as important as technology.

Daniel T. Jones
Monmouth, United Kingdom

COVER NOTE

The character on the cover and shown here is the kanji (Japanese) or hànzì (Chinese) that represents the concept of human. It is composed of just two strokes, resembling a person standing or walking.

It is a reminder that, at the heart of both Lean Thinking and Agile, there is "respect for humanity," seeing the potential in every person, and working hard at creating an environment where people can realize their potential, be creative, and truly enjoy their work.

AUTHORS' NOTE

To provide context to readers curious about our story, we have included this optional section, which is not essential to understand the remainder of the book.

OUR JOURNEY

Escaping the Corporate World

On March 4, 2006, Roger Federer defended his title against Rafael Nadal in the Dubai Tennis Championship final. By then, Federer had established his dominance in tennis. As the world's number one for two years, his winning streak of 81 out of 85 games at the time made him almost unstoppable. Almost, that is, but for one rising star, Rafael Nadal, who in only three encounters had already defeated Federer twice. For tennis superfans, this fourth encounter in Dubai was the turning point that would show whether Nadal's victories had been a fluke or the beginning of one of the most intense rivalries in tennis history.

Benoît is a tennis superfan, and he didn't want to miss witnessing this. Unfortunately, watching the game required access to a niche pay TV channel that Benoît didn't have. Undaunted, he set off to find a place with the right subscription and a willingness to show the game. In a big city with hundreds of bars, this shouldn't be too difficult, he thought.

As he wandered around a neighborhood known for its large number of bars, Benoît started to worry. The venues he visited either didn't have the channel, were not keen on showing sports in the middle of the afternoon, or were already showing another game. By the time the game had started, Benoît was still searching. Despair was setting in.

Two hours after leaving his apartment, Benoît finally walked past the Bombardier, a quintessentially English pub that shared his passion for sports and was showing the game on one of its screens. Relieved, Benoît could finally sit down and enjoy the game, but by then he had missed the first half. After the game, he called Fabrice to share his frustration.

We convinced ourselves that this was a problem that an internet startup could and should solve. Close to finishing our studies, we jumped on this opportunity to escape the corporate world that was waiting for us and launched Allomatch.com, now part of Fanzo.com, a bar finder website for every sports fan who's ever asked, "Does anyone know a place that will be showing . . . ?"

Fabrice built the very first version of Allomatch.com overnight. At the time, we didn't know anything about professional software engineering technologies nor methodologies. We also didn't have much money or time, as we were still students. We focused on delivering value as rapidly and cheaply as we possibly could.

The first version was hacked together using Joomla, one of the open-source content management systems available at the time. We then very quickly onboarded customers, because the most time-efficient way to have the information about when a bar was showing a game was to ask the bar owners to provide it themselves every week. Once the first few early adopters had agreed to contribute their information, we nurtured these precious relationships by quickly updating the product to show them we took their feedback seriously.

Finally, we turned the product into a paid subscription early on, to reassure ourselves that there were customers ready to pay for our new service before we committed to the project full-time. During the first two years, Allomatch.com's focus on delivering value as efficiently as possible made us very user-centric and iterative in our product approach, which helped us sign up hundreds of clients and grow the traffic to millions of visitors a year.

Our initial, quick iterative approach didn't prevent us from hitting two obstacles, one on the tech side and another on the business side.

On the tech side, after two years the technical debt caught up with us. When Fabrice started coding Allomatch, he was an inexperienced graduate student. As a result, Allomatch did not follow much industry best practice. The accumulation of quick and dirty iterations made every new addition difficult to build. We almost apologized to the new developers we hired.

We were not the only ones in the world facing these issues at the time. An innovation was spreading in the web industry to address that exact technological bottleneck: open-source MVC (model–view–controller) frameworks. These were free, prebuilt architectures: Django for Python, Ruby on Rails for Ruby, and Symfony for PHP. They were accessible to any developer, even junior ones. It was like wanting to build a house and having somebody give you solid foundations for free. For engineers like us, it was easy to understand the value of such a framework: it accelerated development and provided the guide rails that helped us avoid creating a spaghetti codebase.

After four months of hard work, the codebase was finally migrated to Symfony, and it was night and day on the tech side. The framework delivered on its promise to make evolutions easier to implement and ensure better quality with its built-in best practices. Overall, Symfony allowed Allomatch's codebase to grow for another 12 years without needing a rewrite.

The second obstacle was on the business side. After two years, Allomatch was not generating enough revenue to sustain itself. Our focus on efficiency had kept our costs low, but we were barely earning enough to be profitable. Our quick iterative approach had helped us sign up more than a hundred clients, but we hadn't taken the necessary step back to realize that we were addressing a too-small market. Despite putting in a lot of effort, we could not find a way to pivot Allomatch to a different, bigger market.

One late evening, walking in the street after work, we talked about our lack of options and worryingly low cash levels. That's when we remembered that a few days before, an entrepreneur we knew had told us he wanted to build his own piece of software to help him scale his business. We had recommended him to someone else, but then realized we had missed a revenue opportunity that could keep the company afloat for a few more months. We called him and convinced him that we could help. Together we built a tech product that was a game changer for his business. It helped him scale much faster by reducing the time it took to serve his clients, from one week to three hours. When a larger player in his industry saw this, the company offered to acquire his business. The product lived on within the acquiring company and continued to generate growth for another decade.

When this first experiment in building tech products for a client ended up being both a thrilling challenge and also a huge success, we saw an opportunity to relaunch ourselves in a new industry. That's how Theodo started: as a tech product builder for startups and small businesses.

Theodo

Finding Theodo's first clients was not particularly hard. Many startups and SMEs needed to build a tech product, lacked the capability to do so, and were struggling to find a provider they could trust. With Allomatch. com as a readily available reference and our successful migration to the Symfony framework, we could demonstrate both our product and tech expertise to prospective clients.

What we did not have was a strong methodology. We tried offering an Agile-only approach, which seemed closest to our experience building Allomatch, but our clients were reluctant to give up the reassurance of up-front specifications and fixed price. So we tried a creative blend of traditional project management with Agile practices. Sadly, that blend combined the worst of both worlds: delayed start because of the long specification phase, teams left to figure out implementation on their own, and misunderstandings discovered at the end.

A project in 2011 illustrated how bad that approach could be. Two brothers came to us to build their online counseling platform. They were passionate about their project and determined to do something meaningful. As it was a new product, we felt it was important to be able to iterate and advised them to use Agile methods for that. But they insisted they knew exactly what they wanted, so we started working on their initial requirements without challenging them very much.

As we built the product, however, their understanding of what they wanted changed. They asked for modifications and new features accordingly, and we reluctantly agreed to unsatisfactory compromises. The budget had been set in stone up front, so each change was additional unplanned work and costs. Even worse, when they finally began to test the market, they realized that the platform as they had imagined it was completely useless. They needed something different and decided to throw away the whole thing. It was a big failure for everyone.

At the end of the project, they invited us out for a drink to debrief. One of the brothers was very blunt and told us that we were good technically, but we had screwed up the product. It was hard to hear and we challenged him: he was the one who had rejected our recommendation to work in a fully Agile way.

We will never forget his answer: "When I go to the doctor, I don't show up with the prescription. You are the expert, and you have to tell me what the course of action is. If Agile was the way to succeed, it was your responsibility to impose it on us."

That discussion was a shock and an eye-opener. He was right, of course. We could not push the responsibility of knowing the right methodology onto our client. If we didn't believe in the way we worked, then it was time we did something about it.

Galvanized by the two brothers' challenge, we decided to radically change our approach with our next clients. We decided to go all-in on Agile and either succeed at making our clients happy or reconsider our commitment to growing a consultancy.

Going All-in on Agile

Deciding to involve the client and iterate on the product to become fully Agile was not that straightforward. Agile was not compatible with our fixed-price business model. If we involved the client and future users during product development and allowed them to ask for changes at every iteration, that would make the initial specifications and corresponding pricing moot after the first few iterations. Our contracts were based on those initial specifications and pricing.

We decided to strengthen our Agile and Scrum expertise by training with Jeff Sutherland, the cofounder of Scrum himself. We wanted to make sure we had a deep enough understanding and the credibility to reassure our clients that with the quality of our implementation, their project would be a success.

We also adapted our business model to align incentives for the client and the tech team, and we started billing by the sprint: a set period of time with a defined work product. This time and material model ensured we could be Agile on specifications without having to renegotiate the initial contract at every change. It also meant that both parties felt immediate accountability when things took longer than expected and started to address it together. Both parties also felt similarly excited when coming up with an ingenious way to build the same feature in less time.

As a result of these changes, we could invite clients into the development teams in the role of product owner. Our teams previously had sporadic interactions with clients. Now they began to have daily conversations with them, on top of half-day meetings each week as part of our one-week sprints. Every team had a Scrum master in charge of ensuring correct methodology implementation and facilitating conversations between the engineers, who were often younger and reserved, and the clients, who were typically outspoken and more experienced business leaders.

We also began to work with very detailed specifications, but just for the next two or three weeks of work, rather than for the whole project as a waterfall approach requires.

Finally, we increased accountability within the team. We made progress visible by splitting the work in increments of less than a day and using a burndown chart every morning to show whether the team was going faster or slower than its target. This made everyone fully aware of problems the morning after they appeared, during the daily stand-up meeting. We also introduced the discipline of doing a retrospective every time a delay occurred, to learn from the problem and identify potential countermeasures.

The results exceeded our wildest expectations. Demanding as it was, our clients loved this system. They could see the product they wanted being built before their eyes every day. They also liked being part of the team, engaging regularly with our developers and benefiting from their engineering insights. Problems were now solved as soon as they appeared, which let us keep customer satisfaction high. Not only did our clients become much happier, but they were excited to entrust us with a lot more of their projects and recommend us to their networks. We started having more and more inbound clients, thanks to positive word of mouth. Our revenue almost tripled that year. We became vocal advocates of Agile, spreading the benefits we had experienced to many more organizations.

The Growth Challenges That Agile Didn't Solve

This marked the beginning of a long period of fast growth, which created new challenges. We started working on bigger projects. We found it hard to scale Agile to multiple teams collaborating toward the same objective. At the time, "Agile at scale" frameworks like SAFe or LeSS had not yet been released. Some simple ideas had quickly emerged, like coordinating multiple Scrum teams through a weekly meeting of team leaders. Jeff Sutherland, the cofounder of Scrum we had trained with, called this the Scrum of Scrums.[1] But there was no tried-and-tested path for scaling Agile to multiple teams in the way that Scrum and Extreme programming (XP) had been a clear path to implementing Agile in a single team.

While working on bigger software projects, we also discovered a second limit: with more code came bigger quality challenges, but those quality challenges had become less of a focus in the Agile community. Early on in the Agile movement, XP was a leading methodology that put a lot of emphasis on tech quality. For example, XP includes rules on how to code,[2] such as "All production code is pair programmed," "Code the unit test first," "All code must pass all unit tests before it can be released," or "Refactor whenever and wherever possible." Yet the Agile methodologies that spread widely and eventually dominated in the community were those associated with improving delivery, leaving us without much help on our challenges to maintain code quality at scale.

More generally, Agile methodologies didn't provide any guidance on how to run a fast-growing company. The Agile community didn't often discuss how to find and delight customers; recruit, train, and retain talent; maintain quality at scale; or finance growth. These growth-related challenges made us realize that Agile methodologies had their limits when it came to scaling.

We started looking for help on how to scale our tech organization while staying Agile. Through our involvement with the pioneers of the French Agile community, we had many discussions about what worked and what didn't on large software and within large organizations. No one felt they had cracked it. Many had managed to inject Agile principles in large organizations, but they had seen little real effect if the organization was too large and didn't have the "right culture." But we didn't despair. The existence of inspiring companies such as Amazon, Apple, Google, and Tesla had convinced us to continue looking for ways to create that culture.

One day at the Agile Open, a three-day self-organized Agile unconference in the Alsatian countryside, Fabrice met someone who claimed he had found a way. Antoine Contal had tried to apply Agile at scale at a large telecom company. Failing to do so, he had looked for inspiration in the roots of the movement and there had found a framework—Lean thinking—that had worked where previous efforts had failed. His examples resonated with our own experience, so we asked him to give us some guidance. He had quit the large telecom company he was working for to become a Lean coach, so he was in a position not only to share his journey, but also to help us through our own. We jumped on that opportunity to learn more about Lean and agreed to a first coaching session.

The Discovery of Lean

Antoine Contal asked us right away, in true Lean *sensei* style, to not sit in a meeting room but to "go and see" how we were creating value. We looked forward to demonstrating our Agile expertise, in particular one of our recent innovations: the project foam board. Since switching to Agile, every team tracked its progress using sticky notes on the wall, organized in five columns: "Backlog," "Sprint backlog," "Doing," "To validate," and "Done." Not only did that require a lot of wall space for each team; it also prevented the teams from changing location within the office or even more challenging, from bringing their stickies to a meeting outside the office.

After two days of researching solutions and evaluating different options for solving that problem, someone gave us the idea of "foam boards": very large but also very lightweight boards that each team would use as a place to stick its Post-it notes. Now teams could move their boards, and the board became the thing that communicated everything there was to know about a project at a glance. This visibility helped immensely with our "customer collaboration," one of the four key values of the Agile manifesto.

But when Antoine looked at our project boards, something bothered him.

"Are you looking at client satisfaction?"

We said that we were.

"Great. But I can't see it."

We were sending our clients a weekly survey to ask how they felt about the speed of the team and about the collaboration's quality. For some reason, we had not thought about putting that information on the project board, the place we claimed had all the information about the project's status.

"Why don't you stick the information on the project board so that the whole team can see it?" Antoine asked.

That was the first aha moment of our Lean journey. Antoine had seen something that to him was obviously waste and used his Lean coaching skills to make it suddenly visible to us, too.

We did as Antoine suggested. Every week, from that moment onward, the client survey was pinned on the project board, telling the team directly and immediately how the client felt about their work.

This alone would have already been very impactful. Antoine also challenged us to do more than just relying on "Individuals and interactions," the first value of the Agile Manifesto, to get problems solved. Leaving people alone to sort out their problems might work with experienced teams, but what about less experienced ones? Antoine showed us a number of problem-solving techniques our teams could learn to solve the problems surfaced by the weekly client forms, or any other problem they faced. He also convinced us of the importance of management supporting teams, not by solving their problems but by coaching them as they solved their own problems.

These small changes were game changers for Theodo. They marked the start of our Lean journey. Our client satisfaction on projects improved 20 percent from an already good level over the following two years. Our revenues grew by a factor of 10 over the following four years. We successfully scaled from 12 to 84 hires a year.

Transforming Legacy IT into a Tech Company

With Antoine's help, we developed a reputation for pushing the Agile envelope. Soon enough, serendipity brought us to Bruno, a CIO at a large bank, who was determined to explore what "real Agile" looked like in a large organization. His plan was to partner with a software consultancy at the forefront of Agile, build a few teams who would try their hardest to bring startup velocity to his large IT organization, and then spread it across the organization. It seemed like a perfect match for us. Excited by the challenge and naïve enough to underestimate the hurdles ahead of us, we agreed to show the organization what "good" looked like and build it a mobile app in only six weeks.

Six weeks later, the app was live, but it went against almost every one of the bank's internal IT processes. Delivering the app had required multiple clearances and direct sponsorship at the highest level. It was a great proof of concept, but a solution that relied on getting exceptional permissions from the bank COO was not sustainable. The permissions were temporary anyway, so after a few weeks the app had to come down. The next challenge was to migrate the app to the bank's internal IT systems.

As we started looking into it, we realized the gap was absolutely colossal. We had to move from an on-demand cloud infrastructure to on-premise servers inside a heavily guarded internal network. Rather than provisioning the infrastructure in a few clicks in the cloud, we would have to fill in multiple forms to ask for servers, databases, architectural review, network port openings, and so on. Each process took weeks, and not filing the paperwork correctly could mean restarting the process from scratch.

As daunting as this was, infrastructure and deployment were still the easier part and we could see the end in sight. On the data side, however, we were stuck. We were building a mobile app and therefore needed the data to be accessible from any network—not just the internal one. That went against years of IT security policy. Understandably, the security manager's answer was a plain "no."

It would take more than a year to set up an environment that would let us securely access internal data from a mobile app, and within such an environment, every further iteration would still take weeks to deploy. Actually transferring the code from the developer's machine to the production servers required burning it onto a CD-ROM and crossing the city by train to deliver it.

We had just come back from Velocity Santa Clara, the leading conference on devops and web operations, where we were blown away by the state of the art. Tech leaders from Amazon, Google, Netflix, Etsy, and so on measured success in their number of deployments to production . . . per hour. And these were not small infrastructures: these deployments affected thousands of servers and brought changes to tens of millions of users. By implementing continuous deployment, they could deploy every small iteration directly to production, multiple times an hour. This was a world apart from taking a train to transfer code. We realized that upskilling this large IT organization on Agile methodology would not address the problem. It would never reach the desired agility without a complete overhaul of the underlying technologies.

When we shared our pessimistic outlook with the CIO, he challenged us. Why not use the migration of our six-week app to implement the state-of-the-art deployment pipeline we were talking about? We were enthusiastic about devops, having pioneered the first devops meetup in Paris in 2010, and he was offering us an opportunity to practice real "devsecops": get enthusiastic developers, cynical infrastructure operators, and paranoid security experts to work together to transform a large IT organization. Eighteen months of intense collaboration later, we had migrated the app and built something we once thought impossible: the foundations for on-demand deployment.

As a result, deploying to production went from taking a week at best to a simple push of a button and a few minutes' wait. The newfound agility transformed the organization. It was suddenly able to release apps in less than two months and then continue iterating on them multiple times a day.

Since then, the company has continued to modernize, including building its own, state-of-the-art API management system. This system in particular has been a major step forward in its Agile transformation. It even allowed the firm to start offering its APIs to industry peers with usage-based pricing, becoming a serverless banking provider and generating profit from what used to be a cost center. It's a great demonstration that with the right technological investment and continuous improvement, traditional organizations can catch up with tech-native organizations.

The Study Trip to Japan Bridges the Gap Between Lean and Tech

Our success bringing Agile and Lean to large IT organizations got us noticed in the traditional Lean community, and Benoît shared our story at the International Lean Digital Summit. After the talk, Benoît spoke with Michael Ballé, three-time recipient of the Shingo Prize for Operational Excellence and author of many seminal books on Lean, who challenged us: "What you are doing is great, but it's not real Lean. Lean is jidoka, kanban, kaizen. You are just scratching the surface of the Toyota Production System."

Considering the impact those scratches had had on our organization, we were keen to explore further and learn everything we could about that Toyota Production System (TPS). We read books and pioneered a community of tech founders trying to apply Lean thinking in tech environments. Régis Medina, an XP pioneer who had coauthored *Gestion de projet eXtreme Programming*, the first book about Agile in French, helped us. He brought his combined understanding of tech, Agile, and Lean principles.

But only when we got invited to a Lean study trip in Japan did we realize how far the Lean practiced in Japanese factories was from ours. We saw the insane levels of quality and reactivity that was achieved, which was inspiring but also daunting. This was way beyond anything we had seen in the tech industry.

During that trip, we talked with Michael Ballé and Régis Medina about bridging the gap and decided to embark on this journey together. Michael and Régis started coming to our office for monthly Gemba walks. Over the following years we built the deeper understanding that let us adapt Lean thinking to our tech organization.

A Firsthand Experience of Lean Resilience

We tested the benefits of our approach when headwinds arrived in 2019. At the time, we employed around 300 people and had been growing very quickly for years. Although we had a strong reputation, word was also getting around that we were never available. Blinded by our success, we hadn't seen that this was slowly affecting the demand for our services, until two large clients faced a crisis at the same time and their boards decided they had to cut all their providers at once. Not only did we lose a lot of business almost overnight, but we realized that the high demand that would have allowed us to replace those clients quickly a few years earlier was no longer there. We had no reaction plan, and we were at a size where asking everyone to follow the Agile value of "responding to change" would not provide enough guidance in a stressful moment. It was a wake-up call that we should have built more flexibility into the organization.

But it was also an opportunity to see the value of the work we had started with Michael Ballé on introducing TPS within Theodo. One example was on the commercial side: Michael had quickly seen during his go and sees that our lead time in fulfilling customer demand was too high, a clear sign of inflexibility, and had urged us to make the problem visible by introducing a kanban board in the commercial team. This helped shift the sales culture from believing there was no problem and having a one-size-fits-all sales process to realizing we were not serving our future clients fast enough and we should tailor our answers to fit each client's needs. While everything was going well, this seemed like a good way to accelerate the sales team's progression. But when the growth crisis hit us, this newly acquired flexibility proved key in allowing us to rebound fast. The sales team was better equipped to adapt to clients and tailor our services to fit their needs. We only grew 10 percent in 2019, but rebounded to 30 percent in 2020, climbed to 50 percent in 2021, and stayed profitable the whole time.

Capturing Our Learnings

Ten years after discovering Lean thinking, we have accumulated a unique experience in combining digital technologies with both Agile and Lean methodologies. We've spent 15 years in the tech industry, continuously adopting the innovations of leading tech companies on the products we build, and 12 years of honing our Agile methodology on hundreds of tech products, small and large, for clients in every industry. For 10 years, we have used Lean thinking to scale our organization from 10 people and $1 million revenue to 700 people and $100 million revenue.

We were inspired by the many stories of organizations that had succeeded and were lucky to meet amazing pioneers from the Agile, devops, and Lean communities. We adopted and adapted the different principles we learned about to the reality of our own organization.

We thought that it was time to share our experience. To capture our learnings, we identified four guiding principles that helped us scale our tech organization while maintaining an Agile culture. In this book, we want to share these principles, why they work, and how you can embed each of them in the culture of your tech organization.

PART ONE

Scaling an Agile Culture

THE AGILE MANIFESTO
DOES NOT SCALE

The Reaction to Bureaucracy
in the Software Industry

With Intel 4004, software became an industry.

The beginning of the software industry can be traced back to Intel's 1971 invention of the 4004 microprocessor.[1] This breakthrough accelerated computer adoption and turned software from a niche product to the mass-market offering we know today. The software industry boom created a need for increasingly bigger projects delivered by increasingly bigger teams, which in turn created a need for more coordination.

Soon enough, bureaucracy came to the rescue, repurposing project management methods from construction and manufacturing and adapting them to large software projects. By 1985, the U.S. Department of Defense had codified this kind of approach in DOD-STD-2167A, stating that "the contractor shall implement a software development cycle that includes the following six phases: Software Requirement Analysis, Preliminary Design, Detailed Design, Coding and Unit Testing, Integration, and Testing." This came to be known as the "waterfall model," which seemed to meet the needs of large organizations for simple and replicable processes.

Frustrations with Waterfall

A method that had originated in manufacturing and construction had little chance of being well suited for software; indeed, the waterfall model has some fundamental issues when applied to software. It completely disenfranchises both product engineers, who design the software but don't get to build it, and coders, whom it asks to write code without any context. It focuses almost entirely on the non-value-added parts of the work—preparing and verifying—and barely addresses the step in which the product is actually built, that is, when software is written. It is also based on the fundamental misconception that IT systems can be fully described with specifications before coding starts. If specifications could capture the whole behavior of the target software, we would be able to generate software directly out of those specs and developers would be writing specifications rather than code. Though artificial intelligence (AI) innovation might soon allow this, until now programming languages have been the best way to fully describe what software should do. This misconception of waterfall causes a lot of waste, with different teams trying to fully describe the target software product three times: in the detailed specifications, in the code, and yet again in the testing suite used to check that the code matches the specifications.

Revolt of the Agile Manifesto

In the early 1990s, some software pioneers began to turn against this way of thinking. They each came up with different ways of addressing the waterfall model's shortcomings, all based on the idea of empowering small, multifunctional teams. Scrum, created by Jeff Sutherland and Ken Schwaber in 1995, was the most structured of these approaches.

In 2001, 17 of these pioneers met at a Utah resort to discuss the commonalities among their different software development methods. In their minds, these represented an alternative to the prevalent waterfall approach—from Scrum to Extreme programming (XP), from rapid application development (RAD) to feature-driven development. According to participant Jim Highsmith, many doubted that the participants in this group would ever agree on anything substantive.

But they did, because they all shared a deep rejection of the "Dilbertesque organization," the name Highsmith gave to the bureaucratic ways of working described in the comic strip Dilbert.[2] The group identified four common values at the core of their approaches and combined them to develop the Manifesto for Agile Software Development.

That manifesto captured the essence of what makes a team of software engineers high performing, once they're free from bureaucracy. Agile quickly became incredibly popular, first with software engineers and soon across industries, because it captured the frustration with bureaucracy that we have all experienced as employees or customers.

The World Wants Agile at Scale

Among the early adopters of Agile methodologies in the 2000s were booming tech companies like Amazon, Google, and Netflix. They disrupted entire industries, thanks to an incredible pace of innovation, orders of magnitude faster than their competition. For outsiders, the secret behind their neck-breaking speed was hard to grasp, but one thing was clear: they were "more Agile." That helped convince most business executives of the need to become Agile; they were keen to catch up before being disrupted themselves and Agile looked like the way to become more innovative and less bureaucratic. By 2017, a Deloitte survey reported that 94 percent of companies said "agility and collaboration" were critical to their success.[3] That so many large organizations around the world would make understanding and adopting Agile a top priority is an outcome that the 17 authors of the Agile manifesto had likely not expected and probably didn't want in the first place, given their focus on small teams.

The fact that the Agile manifesto had never been meant for large organizations didn't prevent many consultancies from responding to the huge demand for "Agile at scale." Of the many invented solutions, the most widely adopted is The Scaled Agile Framework®, also known as SAFe®. In 2021, according to Gartner, SAFe® was used by more than 1 million practitioners and adopted by 20,000 enterprises.

SAFe Scales Something, but It's Not Agile

With 20,000 enterprises using it, SAFe must definitely scale. But the Agile pioneers were never convinced that it could succeed in making large-scale software organizations truly Agile. Indeed, many of the original Agile manifesto authors have been negative about SAFe. Ron Jeffries took the training and found it "isn't really Agile in its heart."[4] Ken Schwaber called it "unSAFe and suffocating."[5] Mike Beedle said that SAFe "violates the values of the Agile manifesto." Martin Fowler called it "Shitty Agile for Enterprises."[6] Even within the bureaucratic environment of the U.S. Department of Defense, the chief software officer of the U.S. Air Force strongly discouraged the adoption of SAFe in 2019 because of its excessive resemblance to waterfall.[7]

Tellingly, no successful Silicon Valley tech company has adopted SAFe. One notable exception was Fitbit, where 12 teams adopted SAFe in 2015. The case study of that adoption praises the record number of products released in 2016, thanks to increased velocity,[8] but forgets to mention that 2016 is also the year that Fitbit lost 75 percent of its value,[9] which it never recovered.

Why is SAFe failing so hard at being endorsed by Agile pioneers and Silicon Valley startups as a solution to scale Agile?

Because despite its multiple attempts to respond to its critiques, it achieves scale in a way that makes it impossible in practice to consider the result Agile.

The first issue is adaptability, the essence of agility. The *SAFe 4.5 Reference Guide* has 816 pages of prescriptive practices, enough pages to justify creating a "distilled" version of *only* 315 pages. Among these practices are many synchronization rituals: coach sync, product owner sync, product manager sync, Agile Release Train sync, Release Train Engineer sync, architect sync, portfolio sync. . . . Planning rituals also abound: two-day program-increment plannings, release management meetings, system demos, pre- and post-program-increment planning, solution demos, and so on. All this is to ensure coordination through a large organization and on-time product delivery every 8 to 12 weeks. This amount of planning and synchronizing means that the teams end up swamped in the bureaucracy of delivering what the organization decided should be built. They are in no position to learn whether this thing is actually still valuable to the customer nor adapt accordingly.

The second issue is autonomy. SAFe's multiple layers of decision-making—a portfolio level, a solution train level, a release train level, and a team level—leave teams on the ground with little decision-making room.

Finally, it's hard to imagine such an implementation actually allowing the team direct contact with its customers, despite the stated objective. In practice, the distance between the engineers and the customer prevents teams from working on product value. They end up merely implementing features from a backlog.

SAFe is far from the Agile ideal of adaptable teams empowered to build valuable software.

The Values in the Agile Manifesto Don't Scale

To scale Agile, we don't need a large, multilayered delivery framework. We need guiding principles that can adapt and be relevant in all the contexts encountered in a large organization and help scale while staying true to the Agile ideal. As Ken Schwaber puts it, "Values and principles scale, but practices are context sensitive."[10]

Unfortunately we can't build on the values of the Agile manifesto, because those values are not scalable. The four values of the manifesto are excellent at capturing the essence of what makes an Agile team great, but they were never meant for scaling outside the context of a team or a small organization. To illustrate this point, let's run the thought experiment of scaling all four values of the Agile manifesto, one by one, to very large organizations.

Individuals and Interactions over Processes and Tools

The first value of the manifesto, "individuals and interactions over processes and tools," reminds us that great Agile teams create value by combining individual talents through rapid interactions. The manifesto maintains that their work should not be hampered by useless processes and tools, like the ones we find in the wasteful bureaucracies of a lot of large companies.

The problem is that when you start scaling individuals and interactions, the number of potential connections between people grows faster than the number of people. A team composed of Alice, Bob, and Charlie only has three possible connections: Alice-Bob, Alice-Charlie, and Bob-Charlie. A team of 100 individuals, however, will have a staggering 4,950 possible connections, and a large corporation employing 100,000 people will have around 5 billion. This creates a real challenge in an environment in which creativity and coordination rely primarily on ad-hoc interactions between individuals.

Robert I. Sutton, professor of management science at the Stanford University School of Engineering and a researcher in the field of evidence-based management, points to Google: "When Google got up to about 400 people, Larry Page started longing for the good old days when they didn't have all these annoying managers around," Sutton says. "So he got rid of all of them, because he's Larry Page and he could, but suddenly he had one executive with 100 engineers reporting to him. That didn't last very long."[11]

The value "individuals and interactions over processes and tools" does not scale once the organization is too large for all possible connections between individuals to stay manageable.

Working Software over Comprehensive Documentation

The second value of the Agile manifesto, "working software over comprehensive documentation," puts the emphasis on doing the work rather than documenting it.

There are actually two ideas here. First, we need software that works for users, not long specs to reassure managers. Second, software should be delivered early and often, to confront it with reality, learn, and iterate, rather than overinvest in up-front design and waste time validating every decision far from reality.

The 1990s saw new techniques that made it easier to iterate, such as scripted database migrations,[12] promoted by Martin Fowler in his 2003 article "Who Needs an Architect?,"[13] and automated tests that reduced the cost of quality assurance. However, both ideas start showing limits when software scales in usage and complexity.

Software that passes regular inspections during development will still surface rare bugs in the hands of thousands of users. And delivering frequently will not help coordinate dozens of teams to address the cross-dependencies that creep up and inevitably slow down the value flow.

Kent Beck, creator of Extreme programming and coauthor of the Agile manifesto, shares an example on Facebook of these two issues at very large scale: "Two services shared the same physical rack. One service changed its backup policy from incremental backups to complete backups. These backups saturated the network switch located on top of the rack, causing the second service to fail." Despite working on two very different services and being completely unaware of each other, the two teams were actually linked by a dependency so that one team's decision to change its backup policy caused the other team's service to fail.

The value of "working software over comprehensive documentation" does not scale once the software reaches the size and usage at which it becomes a complex system. Both controlling quality from the outside and coordinating teams by delivering frequently become insufficient to avoid releasing defects while iterating fast.

Customer Collaboration over Contract Negotiation

The third value of the Agile manifesto, "customer collaboration over contract negotiation," highlights the importance of nurturing trust not just within the team, but also with the customer. This addresses a common problem of bureaucracies: they become so focused on their inner workings that they forget who the customer is and end up acting against their own customers.

Ron Jeffries, cocreator of Extreme programming, says that forgetting the customer doesn't happen in an Agile organization if "the customer (a business decision maker who knows what is needed and can decide priorities) is 'on site' with the team." In our experience at Theodo, embedding the customer within the software development team is indeed incredibly powerful. This practice can even be extended to end users, by arranging for the development team and its customers to regularly meet with actual users. This helps everyone clarify what value means to end users and settles a lot of the potential debates that might otherwise exist within the team, thus removing the need for long negotiations.

However, in an organization with hundreds or thousands of people, not everyone can be in direct contact with the customer, making such collaboration very difficult. In large projects the customer is also often not unique, but actually composed of multiple stakeholders with varying preferences. It becomes very hard to determine the right product to build, just by collaborating with them.

The value of "customer collaboration over contract negotiation" does not scale once the organization reaches a critical mass where teams are too far from the customer or where the customer is itself a large organization (or collection of organizations and/or individuals) struggling to provide clarity on the desired value.

Responding to Change over Following a Plan

The last value of the Agile manifesto is "responding to change over following a plan." It is there to remind us that agility is about being resilient: being able to regularly see how the situation is changing and adapt accordingly.

Continuing to follow a plan despite changed circumstances is perhaps bureaucracies' biggest shortcoming. When faced with an unexpected situation, a bureaucracy prefers to escape the difficulty by sticking to the original process.

This inability to respond constructively to change is one of the key reasons behind the failure of most large, complex software projects. The projects that do succeed are those that are carried out by teams that are not afraid to take change in their stride, as Martin Fowler observes: "We've examined plenty of successful projects and few, if any, delivered what was planned in the beginning, yet they succeeded because the development team was agile enough to respond again and again to external changes."[14]

But responding to change is very difficult in a larger organization. Even when a few teams do respond constructively to change, that doesn't help the organization make strategic turns. And leadership able to initiate those strategic turns lacks the context it would need to make good decisions quickly. As a result, response to change in large organizations is either smart but localized, or global but ill-defined.

The value of "responding to change over following a plan" does not scale once the organization becomes too large for the leadership team to carry the responsibility of every decision and localized initiative is no longer impactful.

Large Organizations with Agile Cultures Exist

The values in the Manifesto for Agile Software Development were never designed for large organizations and are not helpful when trying to scale an Agile culture.

But that doesn't mean that "Agile at scale" does not exist or that an organization can't be both large and Agile. Indeed, many companies have scaled successfully while avoiding most of the bureaucracy we expect in organizations of a similar size. Take two outstanding examples: the Linux kernel development community, bringing together 20,000 developers to invest their free time in creating the world's most critical operating system, and Buurtzorg, a Dutch healthcare provider that scaled to more than 15,000 nurses as a network of self-managed teams. No one can argue that these two organizations are not both very large and still very Agile.

These two organizations are not the exceptions that prove the rule. In just a few years, tech scale-ups have caught up with large incumbents that had needed decades to get to similar market shares in their industry. These tech scale-ups have demonstrated agility at scale, maintaining fast-paced innovation and delivering good-quality products, despite growing to have some of the biggest market capitalizations in the world. They may have become more bureaucratic than the Linux kernel development community or Buurtzorg, but they are still much more Agile than their traditional competitors.

What makes those organizations Agile, even though they have no connection to the manifesto? We decided to find out by digging into the origins of Agile and particularly Scrum, the leading influence on today's understanding of Agile.

THE LEAN TECH
MANIFESTO

Looking for Agile and Scalable Principles

Scrum has become the most popular Agile methodology, with 80 percent of Agile software teams using a version of it.[1] It is also one of the first. Ken Schwaber and Jeff Sutherland created it in the early 1990s when, looking for alternatives to the bureaucratic approaches to software development they were so fed up with, they both independently stumbled upon the "Scrum" approach described by two Japanese professors, Hirotaka Takeuchi and Ikujiro Nonaka, in the 1986 *Harvard Business Review* article "The New New Product Development Game."[2] When Schwaber and Sutherland met and realized they had worked on similar ideas, they joined forces to solidify their methodology and then published their results at the 1995 OOPSLA conference[3] and in the 2001 book *Agile Software Development with Scrum*.

Scrum Was Inspired by Japanese Ways of Working

Scrum as we know it was therefore inspired by the research of Takeuchi and Nonaka on the management techniques best suited for innovation projects. As part of their research, the authors studied a number of innovative Japanese manufacturing companies and identified a common approach across their best-performing innovation teams. Since the teams were all small and tight-knit, Takeuchi and Nonaka used the metaphor of a rugby scrum to describe the way they worked.

Scrum's origins are therefore found in Japanese manufacturing companies' innovative ways of working. To better understand what makes those ways of working innovative, we need to dig into the revolution that happened in Japanese manufacturing after World War II.

The Japanese Manufacturing Revolution and the Emergence of "Lean Principles"

It's hard to imagine a time when "made in Japan" was synonymous with bad quality. But until World War II, the Japanese had leveraged most of their capital and their best managers, engineers, and materials to serve their country's imperial ambitions and to make their military hardware competitive with that of Western powers. As a result, consumer exports were of terrible quality back then.

Faced with the challenge of rebuilding their shattered economy after the war, Japanese businessmen turned to two American quality experts for help: W. Edwards Deming and Joseph M. Juran. The two men typically gave U.S. lectures only to quality managers, but in Japan, Juran recounts speaking to 140 chief executives from the largest manufacturing companies in the country.[4] Similarly, at Deming's 1950 lectures, the top industrial managers attending represented around 75 percent of the country's industrial capital base at the time, including top Japanese industrialists of the likes of Akio Morita, the cofounder of Sony Corporation.[5] Adopted by the top executives and propelled by a tremendous effort to catch up on quality, Deming's and Juran's ideas contributed to a revolution in Japanese manufacturing.

By the 1970s, Japanese cars were higher quality and more fuel efficient than American cars, and when the oil embargo shifted American consumers away from oil-guzzling vehicles, they took over a large chunk of the market. That's when the world realized something had happened in Japan and started to take a keen interest in Japanese ways of working.

To understand why Japanese cars were so superior, a research team at the Massachusetts Institute of Technology led by Daniel Jones, Daniel Roos, and James Womack compared 90 automobile assembly plants in 14 countries. In 1990, they published their findings in the seminal book *The Machine That Changed the World*. They observed that Japanese factories, especially Toyota's, had a radically different way of thinking about how people work together to create value. This let them achieve much higher quality and resilience at considerably lower costs.

To describe the Toyota approach they had observed, Jones, Roos, and Womack decided to use the term "Lean," coined in 1988 by John Krafcik, an MIT graduate student who worked as a researcher for Womack. In their 1996 book *Lean Thinking*, they called the principles at the heart of that approach "Lean principles." Lean principles triggered a revolution in the car industry, with most companies around the world looking to adopt them in a bid to catch up with the Japanese. They also started influencing other industries, including tech.

The Adoption of Lean Principles in Tech

Before Lean principles influenced Scrum and Agile, Apple's Steve Jobs was one of the very early adopters in the tech industry.

Steve Jobs Learning Lean Principles from Juran

When he launched Apple with cofounder Steve Wozniak, Steve Jobs brought his obsession for detail to product development, helping Apple garner a reputation for quality. However, as Apple scaled and John Scully replaced Jobs as CEO, that passion for high-quality engineering began to fade. It wasn't very long before Apple had significant quality problems, notably a defective line of monitors and some infamous combustible portable computers.

In 1985, Jobs, who had been fired from Apple, launched a new company, NeXT, producing high-end workstations that catered to a niche audience of researchers and academics. It's on a NeXT workstation, for example, that in 1990 Tim Berners-Lee invented the World Wide Web and developed the first browser for it.

At NeXT, trying to figure out a way to scale quality, Jobs became interested in the Japanese approach and hired Juran to help out. Juran taught Jobs Lean principles and inspired him with his "optimistic humanism": his conviction that if given the opportunity, anyone can change and improve a company. In a 1990 interview, Jobs talked about the excitement he felt working with Juran and the impact this interaction had on NeXT's ways of working.[6] He highlighted in particular two cultural changes that Juran brought to NeXT. First, the company adopted a scientific approach to doing things, making sure there was an explanation for doing anything a certain way and people were given the opportunity to question it. Second, leadership gave authority to the people who were in the best position to decide how to improve their ways of working: the people actually doing the work.

In a twist of fate, Apple decided to acquire NeXT to be Apple's new operating system NeXTSTEP in 1996, after struggling for years to develop a new operating system internally. As part of the acquisition deal, Steve Jobs was back at Apple and a few months later reappointed as CEO. Over the following 14 years, Apple's market cap grew by more than 100 times under Jobs's leadership. That's a testament to his success at reestablishing Apple's reputation for excellent-quality products while growing it into the largest company in the world, an incredible application of Juran's teachings and an inspiration for other tech entrepreneurs.

Jeff Bezos Learning About Toyota and Adopting Lean Principles

Jeff Bezos, Amazon's founder, is another high-profile tech entrepreneur who leveraged Lean principles. In *Working Backwards*, Colin Bryar, who was Bezos's chief of staff from 2003 to 2005, writes that Bezos had learned about the Toyota approach to quality control and continuous improvement in the early 2000s. Bryar shares a story that illustrates this during one of Bezos's stints in customer service.

At Amazon every executive, including Jeff Bezos, has to work in customer service for a few days every two years. During one of these sessions, Bezos saw an experienced customer service agent take a call and with very little context immediately guess which product the customer was complaining about. Being on the front line, the agents knew which products had recurring issues. But all they could do about the problems was offer the customer a discount, make an apology, and ship a replacement.

That's when Bezos thought about Toyota's *Andon*. At Toyota, any operator on the assembly line who notices a quality problem can pull the "Andon cord" and stop the entire line so the issue can be fixed right away. If the workers are unable to solve the quality problem themselves, a team of specialists swarms to the cord-puller's station, troubleshoots the issue, and develops a fix so that the error never occurs again. Inspired by the idea, Bezos immediately requested an Andon for Amazon called "the big red button." It lets customer service agents instantly stop Amazon.com from selling a particular product until the category manager and team have resolved the recurring issue with that particular product.

Amazon's big red button, just like Toyota's Andon cord, has improved quality by helping surface serious issues as soon as they are noticed and empowering people on the front line by providing them with the right tools to solve problems. These two ideas are now part of Amazon's leadership principles.[7] "Leaders ensure that defects do not get sent down the line," and "Leaders ask themselves: Are my fellow employees [. . .] empowered?"

Bezos further accelerated the deployment of Lean principles at Amazon with the 2006 appointment of Marc Onetto, a veteran Lean executive, as senior vice president of worldwide operations and customer service at Amazon.[8] His impact can be felt in Bezos's 2008 letters to shareholders, where he shares his excitement with discovering waste and looking for its root causes: "Everywhere we look (and we all look), we find what experienced Japanese manufacturers would call 'muda' or waste. I find this incredibly energizing." And then, "At a fulfillment center recently, one of our Kaizen experts asked me, 'I'm in favor of a clean fulfillment center, but why are you cleaning? Why don't you eliminate the source of dirt?' I felt like the Karate Kid."[9]

Lean Principles in the Agile Software Community

Lean thinking has been inspiring the Agile community for a while now. Many books have contributed to this, including Mary and Tom Poppendieck's *Lean Software Development* (2003), Donald Reinertsen's *The Principles of Product Development Flow: Second Generation Lean Product Development* (2009), Steven Bell and Michael Orzen's *Lean IT* (2010), Eric Ries's *The Lean Startup* (2011), and *Lean Enterprise: How High Performance Organizations Innovate at Scale* by Jez Humble, Barry O'Reilly, and Joanne Molesky (2015).

The devops movement is also a great adaptation of Lean principles to the software production flow. *The Phoenix Project: A Novel About IT, DevOps, and Helping Your Business Win*, one of the first books on devops, includes the story of an IT leader visiting manufacturing plants to study Lean production and use it as a source of inspiration to improve his IT operations.

So why hasn't every large organization trying to scale Agile directly embraced Lean principles?

It's probably because Lean has not been associated enough with the challenges of scaling a tech organization. Lean is still strongly associated with the manufacturing industry. There is a strong expertise gap in translating those principles in a way that is easily understood by tech professionals. Even Marc Onetto, Amazon's most senior Lean expert, admits his limited experience: "Perhaps the biggest challenge I see is the application of Lean management principles to software creation. [. . .] I've tried to address the problem, and some of Amazon's computer-science engineers have looked at it, but it is still one of the biggest challenges for Lean."[10]

Lean has also been strongly associated in the Agile community with *Lean Startup*, Eric Ries's bestselling book on product innovation that popularized the concept of minimum viable product (MVP) and validated learning through continuous experimentation. Though *Lean*

Startup is indeed an interesting application of Lean principles on the innovation side, it created an image of Lean as being a method dedicated to product innovation in early-stage startups.

After 10 years growing a software company using Lean thinking, we can confirm that confining Lean thinking to manufacturing or product innovation is a misconception. By helping us scale while maintaining an Agile culture, Lean showed that it applies very well to our creative industries, where creating better solutions requires everyone to collaborate and contribute their best thinking. While it has also been very helpful in early-stage product innovation, it has been most valuable in helping us address the challenges of scaling from $1 million to $100 million in revenue.

To help more tech organizations adopt Lean principles, we want to share how we adopted them and combined them with tech innovation to scale our software organization. We captured that experience in four guiding principles that for us are the best way to expand the four principles of the Manifesto for Agile Software Development at scale.

THE LEAN TECH MANIFESTO

We are uncovering better ways to scale tech organizations by doing it and helping others do it. Through this work we have come to value:

VALUE FOR THE CUSTOMER
over "customer collaboration over contract negotiation"

A TECH-ENABLED NETWORK OF TEAMS
over "individuals and interactions over processes and tools"

RIGHT-FIRST-TIME and JUST-IN-TIME
over "working software over comprehensive documentation"

BUILDING A LEARNING ORGANIZATION
over "responding to change over following a plan"

In the next parts of the book, we will explore how you can embed these principles into the culture of your organization to help it scale better and maintain an Agile culture at scale.

PART TWO

Lead with Value for the Customer

Lead with . . .

Value for the Customer

Right-First-Time

Just-In-Time

Building a Learning Organization

Tech-Enabled Network of Teams

人3

THE BENEFITS PAYMENT CARD STORY

U ntil the early 2000s, the welfare system in the United Kingdom worked on cash payments. More than 17 million people regularly visited one of the nation's 20,000 post offices to collect one or more of the 24 social security benefits given out by the UK Benefits Agency, in cash, for a total of about 760 million payments every year.[1] In May 1996, the Benefits Agency and Post Office jointly decided to replace and modernize this outdated cash-based system. They launched the Benefits Payment Card project.

To build the IT system that would support it, they decided to work with the new private finance initiative framework. They awarded Fujitsu subsidiary Pathway a £1 billion contract (around $1.6 billion at the time), but the framework allowed the Benefits Agency, the Post Office, and Pathway to move beyond the usual, rigid customer-provider relationship and work instead as a tripartite joint venture where they all shared investments and risks. This collaboration let them start the project much more quickly, without having completed and agreed on both purchasers' detailed requirements. It was a good example of the Agile manifesto value "Customer collaboration over contract negotiation," a few years before the Manifesto for Agile Software Development.

In October 1996, only five months after the contract's start, the first version of the system was released and paid child benefits in 10 post offices. The innovative approach had worked. After a few more iterations, the updated version ran in 205 post offices.

However, these initial steps also showed signs that scaling to the 24 existing types of benefits and all 20,000 post offices would be much more difficult than expected. The original target of reaching that goal in 10 months had to be changed, and in February 1997 the three parties agreed to a no-fault replan of the project, which included delaying the full release and increasing investments. The Benefits Agency employed up to 1,100 staff plus consultants to design and implement its part of the system, while Pathway strengthened its project management team and increased staffing and technical resources. At that point, it still seemed that the group had spotted difficulties early enough and that close collaboration would overcome them. Everyone was working hard to make the project successful.

But the project continued to slip, costs threatened to escalate, and the fundamental issue became clearer: the Benefits Agency and the Post Office had two different objectives. The Benefits Agency's main objective was to reduce fraud. The Post Office's objective was to lower costs through automation and create new commercial opportunities by extending the system to other customers and products.

The project was at a point where this started creating disputes, further increasing the delays. Security was an example of such disputes: the Benefits Agency had agreed to make exemptions on some of the contracted security features, despite their importance for its fraud reduction objective, to make the initial rollout to 205 offices easier. But now that the Benefits Agency wanted the security features back, the Post Office objected to the negative impact these features could have on the flow of customers through its outlets.

By the end of 1997, the collaborative approach had disappeared and the discussion became contractual. The purchasers blamed Pathway for being in breach of contract, Pathway denied liability, and the Benefits Agency issued the cure notice, which allowed it to terminate the contract. Negotiations continued, but by then the project had stopped moving forward. It was finally canceled in 1999.

The total waste was estimated at £1.3 billion ($2 billion). Of that total, £519 million ($830 million) came from the expected fraud savings that did not materialize. The remainder was made up of written-off IT investments: £571 million ($910 million) at the Post Office, £180 million ($290 million) at Pathway, and £127 million ($200 million) at the Benefits Agency. The parties had successfully shared the risks, but hadn't aligned their objectives to make the project a success.

Auditors declared that divided control was the top reason for the project's failure.[2] The Benefits Agency and the Post Office had tried to address this at the start of the project by agreeing on a memorandum of understanding before signing the contract with Pathway. But once the project had scaled and thousands of people were working on it, the memorandum was not enough to settle disputes around the many complex decisions that had to be made.

A second issue was the lack of care for the end user: the benefit claimant.[3] The solution that new benefit claimants had favored all along was automated bank transfers rather than a "Benefits Payment Card." But it had been rejected at the time because it was politically difficult to accept the potential reduction of traffic in the Post Office network.

For the thousands of people working on the project, these two issues compounded to make success impossible. They were under pressure to deliver a complex IT system with competing objectives. And when trying to navigate between the need to reduce fraud and the need to maintain in the Post Office network, they could not even rely on the best interest of users to arbitrate on the best option possible.

Value for the Customer as a Leadership Principle

The innovative contractual framework adopted by all three stakeholders that enabled "customer collaboration" didn't prevent these two issues. A guiding principle that would have better addressed them is "value for the customer," the first Lean principle Jim Womack and Daniel Jones identify in *Lean Thinking*.

If the Benefits Payment Card project had been led by value for the customer, things would have been very different. A clear definition of value would have addressed the problem of competing objectives better than the collaboration efforts around the "memorandum of understanding." Not just focusing on internal needs, but also providing clarity on what creates the most value for the stakeholders and the citizens, would have helped everyone engage with the project's purpose and better arbitrate the many trade-offs they would encounter.

What does leading with value for the customer mean in practice?

- **Finding value for the customer** with go and see visits on the shop floor, creating a value model, and tackling the fundamentals with the SQDCE (Safety, Quality, Delivery, Cost, and Environment) framework
- **Embedding value for the customer within the organization**, leveraging visual management, and connecting teams to value for the customer, using the right team organization or "team topology"

FIND VALUE
FOR THE CUSTOMER

The Benefits Payment Card project is a cautionary tale reminding us that it's possible for organizations to invest hundreds of millions without clarity on their goals. Unfortunately, this is not a rare occurrence, because clarifying objectives requires not only a leadership team with a good understanding of what is needed, but also agreement on priorities, which is particularly hard if there is no compelling North Star to help arbitrate. This is why focus on the customer is so important: to provide the obvious North Star and help align all stakeholders around the same objectives.

Go and See Where the Work Is Actually Done

Before communicating value for the customer to the whole organization, it's crucial that the leadership team has a deep understanding of what it means in its organization and continuously refine its understanding. This is why the first Lean behavior a leadership team should adopt is scheduling frequent visits to the shop floor, known as the *Gemba* in Japanese, to go and see teams directly working on the organization's product or service.

Regular go and see visits, or Gemba walks, help leaders compare existing mental models with reality on the ground. They come away with a better understanding of what value is actually being created, discover the problems that customers and teams face, and find patterns that can nourish higher-level strategic thinking.

Regular and Predictable Visits

Go and see should entail recurring and predictable visits. The idea behind a go and see is not to surprise teams, and there is no need to worry that the heads-up will give teams a chance to embellish reality or hide problems. Good questions will still arise and lead to interesting insights.

As for frequency, Taiichi Ohno—considered the "father" of the Toyota Production System—used to say, "Toyota managers should be sufficiently engaged on the factory floor that they have to wash their hands at least three times a day." You might not be ready to do three visits a day, so start scheduling visits for at least once a week, preferably more.

How do we make sure the go and see visit is a good investment?

Structured Insight-Looking Questions

Go and see is all about observation. Try looking for instances where things don't go as intended and then ask nonjudgmental questions to the people who do the work. The most interesting conversations often start from what looked initially like a small and exceptional issue, but turns out to be the tip of the iceberg and the opportunity for the people on the ground to share their actual experience.

The first step is to carefully listen to what the team members have to say about the issue. Hold back the temptation to answer right away and instead help them explain their point if it is not well articulated at first.

The second step is to discuss what the observed issues mean, both for the company and for the overall business strategy. This is a good moment for leaders to refine their understanding of value for customers and share it with team members, to hear their thoughts on it.

The third step is to commit to a further investigation of one of the issues observed—not to fix the issue, but to take the time to research and give everyone a much better understanding of what is going on.

These frequent go and see visits will give a much better insight into where value for the customer lies and will be useful for creating a value model.

The Value Model

Value is what makes a product or service meet and/or exceed expectations. These expectations are often unclear, even to the person using the product or service, making it tricky to understand expectations and even trickier to explain them. This is hard to get right. You can still achieve very good results by tracking essential business indicators and iterating on a simple value model.

Essential Business Indicators: Revenue and Customer Retention

Customers vote with their wallets by paying for your product or service when they believe it will meet their expectations. They vote with their feet by not buying it again if it doesn't. Revenue and customer retention are therefore not only the organization's source of sustainability, paying everyone's salary and allowing the organization to invest in the future. They are also the most effective way to measure whether your product is delivering value to your customers.

If your organization is at a very early stage and does not yet generate customer revenue, start charging for your services as soon as possible.

Customer expectations are much higher when they pay than when they don't. With higher expectations comes much more relevant feedback, which in turn helps you reach product-market fit much faster.

Iterating on the Value Model

To go further and structure the search for product-market fit, you can start with a simple value model by answering the following two questions:

- What does the customer want more of?
- What does the customer want less of?

When you have answered these two questions, you can iterate on the product and measure whether or not changes bring it closer to success.

An important point here is that there are two dimensions to product success. Marty Cagan, author of *Inspired* and *Empowered* and a leading voice on product management, calls them "value," for what makes the customer buy or adopt the product, and "viability," for what makes the product thrive within the business.[1] Put differently, we need a value model for the customer and a value model for the stakeholders within the business.

How you'll measure whether the product iterations have brought you closer to success depends on your value model. But customer satisfaction and internal stakeholder satisfaction will be relevant in most cases.

Net Promoter Score for Customers and Internal Stakeholders

Regular customer satisfaction surveys give you qualitative feedback that is key to understanding customer expectations and refining your value model. The organization should particularly focus on every piece of negative customer feedback it receives, because this is where you learn the most about value gaps.

The industry standard measurement of customer satisfaction is net promoter score (NPS). To find NPS, ask customers how likely they would be to recommend your offering, on a scale of 1 to 10. "Promoters" have ratings of 9 or 10, "passives" have ratings of 7 or 8, and "detractors" have ratings of 6 or lower.

Calculate the NPS by subtracting the percentage of detractors from the percentage of promoters, and express the result as an integer from −100 to 100, rather than as a percentage. For example, if you survey four customers and get scores of 10, 9, 7, and 2, your NPS would be 50 percent promoters − 25 percent detractors = 25. As a widespread standard, the NPS helps you find benchmarks and compare yourself against industry peers. It also emphasizes how much more difficult it is to build a promoter base than to create detractors.

A similar survey should also be sent to internal stakeholders. At Theodo, teams have collected feedback from the product manager and their business stakeholders every week, on almost every project, since 2012. This has been key in achieving our high client satisfaction. Collecting internal stakeholders' feedback helps understand the trade-offs between what customers want and what the business needs to ensure the product's viability. It's key to creating great products for the users that are also sustainable for the organization. (See Figure 4.1.)

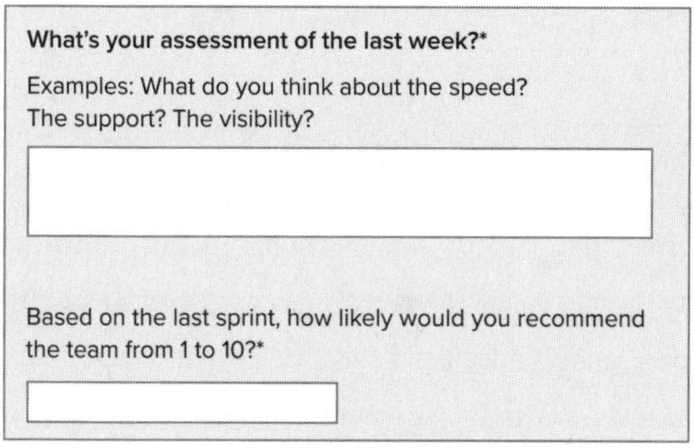

What's your assessment of the last week?*

Examples: What do you think about the speed? The support? The visibility?

Based on the last sprint, how likely would you recommend the team from 1 to 10?*

FIGURE 4.1   Example of a weekly feedback form.

The SQDCE Framework

Next comes hygiene: factors that won't make the product stand out if they're right, but could make the product fail if they're wrong. For that, we use a Lean framework called SQDCE: Safety, Quality, Delivery, Cost, and Environment. Although this framework was first developed for the car industry, it works in any context, so long as you translate the concepts to your own circumstances.

We can find examples of tech products that succeeded despite failing on the SQDCE framework. Microsoft Windows used to be famous for its regular security vulnerabilities and bugs that caused the "blue screen of death," but was still the most popular platform at the time, with 97 percent market share in 2006.[1] But in 2021, Windows had less than a third of market share overall and was absent on mobile.[2] The trust Microsoft lost over 15 years created an opportunity for Apple and Google.

Safety

Safety: Preventing the Impact of Cyberattacks

Safety is the first element in the SQDCE framework. Safety is paramount in the car industry, where safety issues during production or use can cause fatal accidents. With software now taking over more and more critical systems, safety has also become a critical hygiene factor in the software industry.

A spectacular example is the 2017 Equifax data breach. Equifax is a consumer credit reporting agency, collecting and aggregating credit information on more than 800 million individual consumers and 88 million businesses worldwide. This includes sensitive information about individuals, including Social Security numbers, taxpayer IDs, driver's licenses, passport photos, and credit card details. In the hands of a hacker, this information makes it easy to impersonate someone, pay with a stolen credit card, or conduct a more elaborate fraud.

When Mandiant, a leading American cybersecurity firm, audited Equifax's IT systems in March 2017, it found multiple issues, including unpatched systems and misconfigured security policies. It concluded that the data protection systems were grossly inadequate.

Instead of listening to Mandiant's advice, Equifax got into a dispute over the auditing team's lack of seniority.[3] That same month, attackers proved Mandiant right by exploiting a critical vulnerability in Apache Struts, the enterprise Java framework Equifax used on parts of its website that let them execute code on Equifax servers, simply by accessing the customer complaint form. The Equifax IT teams enabled that attack when they didn't patch their vulnerable systems, didn't detect the lack of patching during routine scans, and didn't renew a certificate in their intrusion detection system that could have sounded an alarm.

On July 29, 2017, Equifax's IT teams finally renewed the expired certificate and immediately discovered the attack, but the situation was already grave. Hackers had been exfiltrating data for more than two months, stealing personal information from about 40 percent of the American public, including 200,000 credit card details.[4] This data trove was worth a fortune to criminals, containing all the information they needed to impersonate millions of consumers and commit fraud on a massive scale.

Equifax was heavily fined for that breach, which the U.S. authorities called "entirely preventable." It paid a $1.4 billion settlement to the Federal Trade Commission and committed to invest a mandatory $2 billion in improving security.[5]

Measuring Safety with Penetration Testing

Equifax could have avoided all this by reacting immediately to the issues identified during its March security audit. The "pen test," short for *penetration testing*, is the industry standard to identify security issues. The firm hires an external team to attempt breaking into a company's system and then report back on their findings. The organization offers varying degrees of support, from no help at all to giving testers access to employee accounts and the organization's source code.

We highly recommend conducting regular pen tests, not only to unearth existing issues but also to report on the efficacy of your security precautions.

The problem with reports about security problems is that the best way to decrease the number of issues detected is to simply look less for them. To avoid this conundrum, we recommend categorizing issues by detection stage. For example:

- **A** for issues detected by the IT teams
- **B** for issues detected outside the IT teams, but within the organization
- **C** for issues detected during an audit or pen test
- **D** for issues detected by outsiders
- **E** for issues exploited by criminals

This categorization gives the organization a healthy target: progressively shifting the detection of defects from stages C, D, and E to earlier stages A and B, also known as a "shift-left" approach.

We can apply a similar logic to quality.

Quality

Technical quality is making sure the digital product behaves technically as its users expect. This is why we define defects as any behavior the user doesn't expect, including what is commonly known as "bugs" from code mistakes or infrastructure problems, but also user experience (UX) or naming issues and anything else that generates unexpected product behavior. This wide definition of "defect" means that you will probably have a lot of them and that you will need to categorize them.

A first useful categorization is the "origin of defect": which team was responsible for introducing the defect. Concretely, a UX issue can be linked back to the product/UX team. A confusing wording to the content team. A mistake in the authentication code that disconnected a user to the development team. And a system crash, because of a server's full hard disk, to the infrastructure team. Though multiple teams can be involved, it's about identifying which team can best lead the investigation.

As we proposed for security issues, a second useful categorization is by detection stage:

- **A** if the defect was detected by the developer in a final review, before pushing the code
- **B** if it was detected by someone else on the team or by the continuous integration pipeline, before reaching an internal customer
- **C** if it was detected after reaching an internal customer (product owner, QA, etc.) and before pushing to production
- **D** if it was detected after pushing to production, where it could have affected an external customer, and before receiving a complaint
- **E** if it resulted in a customer complaint

Here again, categorizing by detection stages makes it possible to measure if the organization is successful at detecting defects earlier and progressively shifting the indicator left, away from stages D and E where defects affect the user to earlier stages A and B.

One aspect missing from this definition of quality is performance. Let's consider how to address that.

Delivery

The *D* in SQDCE stands for Delivery or Delay: the speed at which customers get the product they want. In digital, we can apply this to the product's performance, making sure the digital product responds quickly and stays responsive at scale. Two complementary types of tools stand out in measuring performance. The first are tools to analyze a page's performance, such as Lighthouse, created by Google, or Flashlight, its equivalent for mobile.[6] The second are application performance monitoring (APM) tools, which analyze the effect of scaling on the production infrastructure.

A few APM vendors have come together to create the Apdex as a way to provide a standard measure of responsiveness at scale.[7] Similar to

NPS, the Apdex divides a population of users into three groups: "satis-fied," "tolerating," and "frustrated" users. It defines groups according to two thresholds: a response time t under which users are deemed satis-fied and a response time of $4t$ above which users are deemed frustrated. Between t and $4t$, users are deemed tolerating. The Apdex score is equiva-lent to a weighted average of these user counts with weights 1, 0.5, and 0, respectively. This allows us to graph the perceived performance over time (Figure 4.2) and identify when the situation becomes critical.

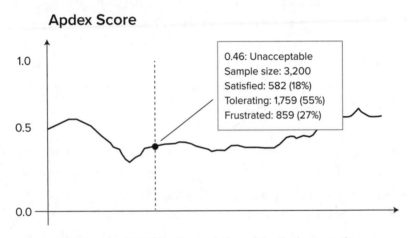

FIGURE 4.2   Graphing the evolution of the Apdex over time.

Once we measure whether a product is safe, is bug-free, and per-forms well, we can finally look at its price.

Cost

The C in SQDCE stands for Cost. This is one topic where the tech indus-try and manufacturing, the sector where SQDCE originated, are at odds. In manufacturing, standard parts that are used in large quantities can be produced in very high volumes, allowing us to lower the unit costs and create significant and strategic cost-reduction opportunities. In the tech industry, reducing costs through production volume is not an option.

The Value Gap Between Best and Worst Teams

People are the main apparent cost in tech organizations. But the real cost in our highly creative industry is the bad design choices that end up introducing defects or missing full value potential. This means two people can have hugely different effects on value, depending on their ability to create great or terrible designs. Steve Jobs believed one of his secrets was that he understood that there was a 25 times difference between a company with the best programmers and one with average programmers, which is why he always insisted on hiring only the best talent.[8] A team able to come up with ingenious ideas that create a decisive edge against competitors can affect company value by orders of magnitude.

Software teams should not focus on reducing costs or increasing code productivity, but on creating the most value by regularly asking themselves these three questions: Are we working on the right topics? Are we doing the work right? Do we have the right indicators to uncover problems?

Developer Velocity

This does not mean that estimating upcoming work and measuring team velocity is necessarily a bad thing. The topic is a source of controversy in the development community, with the #noestimate movement opposing this practice. Indeed, we should measure productivity carefully with two dangers in mind:

1. **Productivity is not the same as value.** Working hard to go faster in the wrong direction will create a lot of frustration and very little value. Or as Elon Musk puts it, "If you're digging your grave, don't dig faster."
2. **Productivity obtained under pressure** rather than through problem solving will harm trust and creativity, destroying opportunities to create value for the customer.

But estimating upcoming work is also a way to think about the work ahead. An environment with enough trust and where value for the customer is well defined makes estimating an opportunity to involve everyone—the product and development teams, and potentially also the design and business teams—in discussing the product and technical architectures. Strong discrepancies in each contributor's estimates represent an opportunity to identify misunderstandings and encourage everyone to look harder for a better architecture or a more ingenious solution that could create more value in less time. More than once, we have seen such conversations end up saving weeks of unnecessary work or come up with a game-changing idea.

There is one place in particular where we can quickly see the impact on costs of the right architecture choices: the cloud infrastructure bill.

Infrastructure Costs

Cloud infrastructures have brought a new model of pay-per-use to a domain that used to be about large one-off investments that the CFO treated as capital expenditure, or Capex.

This has been an incredibly positive development for new digital products. It lets innovative organizations build ambitious cloud infrastructures that can scale very fast once they find a product-market fit, without having to worry about initial investments.

The downside has been the loss of clarity on how much the infrastructure will ultimately cost. The factors affecting the final bill are now spread across every team that has an influence on the product. A product or tech decision can lead to much larger infrastructure use. The cloud provider will happily adapt to this, but it might come as a surprise when the bill is finally totaled.

This has given rise to a new role: finops, a team that analyzes cloud bills and identifies cost-reduction opportunities while working alongside the product and technical teams. The key to a healthy approach to cloud infrastructure costs is to share them with everyone that might affect them. Spending spikes can help point to engineering mistakes or costly product choices, helping teams make better, more cost-aware decisions.

A great example of this is Spotify, which open-sourced its internal tool, called Backstage, with a plugin called Cost Insight.[9] The plugin tracks the infrastructure cost trend, points to spikes, and can also display cost optimizations.

Finally, a side effect of reducing infrastructure costs is the positive effect it can have on the environment.

Environment

The E in SQDCE stands for Environment. Value for the customer is not just about the organization's customers. It's also about the effect the products and services can have on the ecosystem in which we all live. This requires working to minimize the negative effects that products and services can have on the planet, society, and future generations, thinking deeply about how to address them.

Reducing carbon footprint is one such priority for every organization today. A software application's carbon footprint comes primarily from the infrastructure hosting it and the devices required to access it.

On the infrastructure side, cloud vendors such as AWS[10] and Google Cloud[11] have released their carbon footprint calculators, giving customers data on how their usage translates in tons of carbon dioxide. But beyond moving to servers in greener locations, their recommendation is also to optimize usage and therefore costs, because the more you pay, the more energy and servers you are probably using. Tracking and trying to reduce cloud costs is therefore good for the business and for the environment.

On the device side, developers can optimize an app's performance. The better an app performs, the less energy required to run it, and the less it pushes users to update to a new phone to use it.

Finding Value by Combining Intuition and Models

Creating a much better understanding of what and where the value is, starts with going to the "gemba" where the value is created. Through frequent go and see visits, leaders gain valuable ground-level insights into the value being delivered and challenges encountered. This sheds light on misconceptions and opportunities for more value.

These learnings can then be used to create a value model for a shared understanding of value for the customer. This model also helps measure progress, adding to the very useful metrics of revenue, customer retention, customer satisfaction, and internal stakeholder satisfaction.

This model should coexist with the SQDCE framework—safety, quality, delivery, cost, and environment—to maintain the good hygiene standards crucial for long-term viability.

That clearer understanding of value for the customer can act as a powerful North Star. Which leads us to our second challenge: how can we make sure that once value for the customer is well understood by the leadership team, it is also understood by everyone else in the organization?

EMBED VALUE FOR THE CUSTOMER WITHIN THE ORGANIZATION

Visual Management

Visual management is the secret to cooperatively building value for the customer.

It's a critical leadership skill to master, because it:

- Builds trust by sharing key information.
- Creates team alignment. When teams share an understanding of value for the customer, they can align their efforts toward the common goal.
- Supports quick decision-making. Visual management makes it easier for teams to spot problems and fix them.
- Promotes accountability. Clarity around roles, responsibilities, and progress gives team members a sense of ownership.
- Streamlines communication. Information is at hand, reducing the need for long meetings or emails.

You can't decide what your teams think, but you can decide what you show them. That's what makes visual management so powerful. It gives you significant influence over your organization without any need to lecture.

Designing good visual management is far from straightforward. Here are our key learnings to shorten your learning curve.

First, start with value for the customer and make it central. Circle back to it, discuss it, and allow it to evolve. This is the only way to prevent visual management from becoming yet another bureaucratic tool that loses its spark.

Second, carve out significant space for discovery activities. It's both useless and disheartening to do well at the wrong thing, so visual management needs to emphasize the importance of regular tests designed to check whether the organization is on the right track.

Finally, follow the golden rule of visual management: make whatever you display as clear and legible as possible. If viewers have to think hard to understand posted information, your presentation needs improvement. It isn't the reader's job to make an effort to understand. It's the writer's job to deliver information in the simplest, most effective way.

Walls are prime real estate for visual communication, especially at key collaboration locations. Display your visual management in spaces where people meet frequently, such as the kitchen or a large, frequently used meeting room. Give everyone the opportunity to understand what they're working toward by vividly showing them the organization's challenges and the progress it's making.

You might wonder how much confidential information it's safe to post, especially in spaces that are visible to customers and commercial partners. In our experience, there's rarely much harm in sharing key value indicators with your customers and partners, and even potential benefits.

Obeya

To leverage visual management, Toyota has a dedicated Obeya, which means "large room," for all its products. Each product has a large meeting room dedicated to displaying all the key information about it.

The company displays information in part to facilitate good conversations. Frequently shared content includes the definition of value, the plan for creating that value, identified challenges, what the team has learned so far, and current experimental changes.

This content is just as relevant in software. Alan Kay, famous for his pioneering work on object-oriented programming, says, "The first thing I want to see when I visit a software organization is where is your situation room where you can understand what's going on."[1] For him, this is the place where everyone involved in a complex software system can see all the information in the same place, understand the relationships within that system, spot the challenges, and consider how to address them (see Figures 5.1A and B).

FIGURES 5.1A AND B   An Obeya room at AramisAuto.com.

Online Visual Management

It is very hard to re-create an Obeya online. Information displayed on a physical wall is harder to avoid and creates livelier discussions. It is easier to see indicators on an office kitchen wall than to remember to regularly check an online page. Standing next to a physical board with someone else triggers conversations, sparking everyone's curiosity, creativity, or doubts. That's tough to replicate online.

But with Covid-19 normalizing remote collaboration, we've all had to find ways to create digital Obeyas. At Theodo we use Notion as the digital portal where we share organizational and product-specific indicators. We encourage teams to create their own indicator pages and use them as a starting point for weekly or monthly meetings and discussion.

Any online tool that lets teams collaborate on a visual interface can work, as long as it allows enough freedom to customize. Avoid a tool that allows charts and no text, or only charts of a certain type, because it would limit the information you can display.

Visual management is a very effective way to communicate value for the customer to the whole organization. But it does not help teams understand how they contribute to customer value and how to track that contribution. Make that easy by structuring your organization so teams can easily see how they can contribute to customer value.

Teams as the Building Block

Structuring an organization is not about splitting work into steps and individual tasks. The days of Taylorism are gone. Teams have become the building block of an organization. Google calls the team "the molecular unit where real production happens, where innovative ideas are conceived and tested, and where employees experience most of their work."[2]

What Is a Good Team Size?

There are a lot of opinions on the right team size. Scrum says a team should be between three and nine people. Amazon is known for its concept of the "two-pizza team": a group of less than 10 people that can be fed by just two American-size pizzas. Google also uses research to encourage teams of fewer than 10 people.[3]

A more elaborate point of view on team size comes from a Gallup study.[4] According to this study, the optimal team size depends on the manager's competence. After splitting managers into three categories— "high talent," "medium talent," and "low talent"—and measuring their engagement at different team sizes, the study made two very interesting observations. First, high-talent managers can maintain high engagement with their teams at all observed sizes, even in teams of 15-plus people. Second, medium-talent managers can maintain the same high engagement as high-talent managers, but only in teams of fewer than 5 people.

We suggest aiming for small teams when possible. Where bigger teams are necessary, get those teams assigned to the most talented managers.

Once the teams are defined, the next question is how to assemble those building blocks.

The Right Team Topology to Support Value for the Customer

Choosing how to organize teams is somewhat similar to designing the architecture of a large piece of software. It's about understanding the overall system well enough to draw coherent subsystems that both minimize interdependencies and make it easier for everyone to understand both the system and the role of each subsystem in it. This is sometimes referred to as finding the right team topology, after the book *Team Topologies* by Matthew Skelton and Manuel Pais.

When looking to create partitions in an organization—divisions, departments, business lines, and so on—that are coherent and as autonomous as possible, two approaches stand out. The first, often called a "divisional structure," identifies subgroups in customers or product lines and splits the organization around those subgroups.

The second one, often called a "functional structure," identifies subgroups of people within the organization who share common internal expertise.

The 1950s aerospace industry acknowledged these two competing dimensions and tried to address them both by inventing the Matrix Organization (see Figure 5.2).[5]

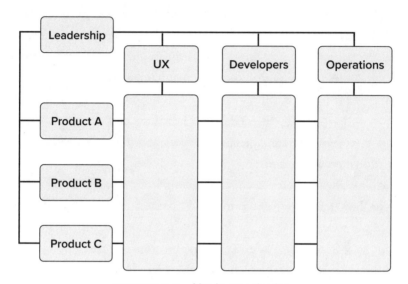

FIGURE 5.2   Matrix organization.

This approach became popular in the late 1970s and early 1980s, but proved unmanageable.[6] Formalized dual reporting led to conflict and confusion, while increasing overall bureaucracy. Organizations have now gone back to acknowledging the need for multiple dimensions, but under a single reporting structure. That requires favoring one dimension over the other, and either choice has trade-offs.

The functional approach has the benefit of being easier for management, because it groups people with similar skills together, but makes cross-functional collaboration harder.

The divisional, or product, approach has the benefit of being customer-centric, clarifying the value stream and therefore making it easier for everyone in the organization to know which customer they are working for. However, it requires duplicating some of the functions and, more importantly, makes it harder to build deep expertise in each function.

In the scaleup world, we have often seen digital structures using the product approach. The divisions in charge of a product line are called "tribes" at Spotify, "swimlanes" at Netflix, and "product areas" at Google.

Apple[7] and Toyota[8] are inspiring counterexamples. Both are functional organizations that have made sure different functions collaborate well along product lines. Apple credits this to decades of promoting to functional leadership positions only those that are very good at collaborating across functions. Both firms are also hardware companies, where the amount of expertise needed to build the final product is much larger than in software development and is less appropriate to small cross-functional product teams.

Whichever option you choose, the important thing is to create clarity on how teams contribute to value for the customer. If we stay on the Agile model of cross-functional product teams that is perfectly relevant in software, we can draw inspiration from the part Marty Cagan dedicated to team topologies in his book *Empowered*. He identifies two fundamental types of tech product teams: "experience teams," which are responsible for how the product value is exposed to users and customers, and "platform teams," which manage services that other internal teams leverage. The best way to create clarity on value for the customer differs according to team type.

Clarifying how experience teams contribute to value for the customer is about giving them responsibilities aligned with customer needs. You might assign each experience team different personas, market segments, or parts of the customer journey.

This is what Spotify has done. Each team, called a "squad," works on a specific part of the user journey (see Figure 5.3).

Similarly, Netflix's swimlanes work on a specific client-focused strategy that's quantified with a metric. For example, the metric for the personalization strategy is the percentage of members who rate at least 50 movies by end of six weeks.[9] Within these swimlanes, product leaders and their cross-functional team of engineers, designers, and data analysts have very

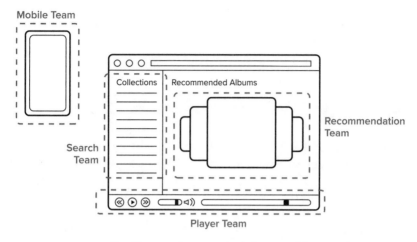

FIGURE 5.3   Spotify squads are assigned parts of the user journey.

strong autonomy, empowered by their clarity on how they contribute to value for the customer.

If the product is small enough, you should endeavor to have only experience teams—that is, teams that work on a client-related topic. On a larger product, some technical challenges will be big enough to justify a dedicated platform team—a team to work on a complex API, for example, or improve the infrastructure on which other teams rely. Its work is not directly for the client, but rather for the internal experience teams. This doesn't mean the platform team can't be connected to value for the customer. Cagan suggests two ways to connect them: shared team objectives and platform-as-a-product objectives.

Shared team objectives happen when a platform team adopts the objectives of the experience teams that rely on their work. This encourages close collaboration and clarity on how the technical work contributes indirectly to the external customer.

Platform-as-a-product objectives happen when the platform team treats the experience team it supports as an internal customer. This is inspired by the many startups that sell technical APIs, such as Stripe and its payment APIs. If a team is working on an internal platform that has the potential to become a technical API, then the internal team can be considered the customer, and value for the customer is redefined accordingly. This turns platform teams into experience teams.

Value for the Customer Empowers Teams

Organizations thrive when they understand the value they want to deliver to their customers and society. The approach Agile uses to clarify value for the customer is very powerful: embed the customer within the team. But it is not scalable.

At scale, the customer is too far away for teams to guess the value just by collaborating with them. In that situation, the leadership team's role is to understand and define value for the customer and then lead the organization with it. To make sure everyone knows how they can contribute to that value, the leadership team needs to communicate it effectively, leveraging visual management for example, and then organize teams so that they can understand and see their contribution firsthand.

But to be fully empowered on contributing to the value, teams need to have enough autonomy. Achieving this at scale is the topic of our next chapter: a tech-enabled network of teams.

PART THREE

Empower People with a Tech-Enabled Network of Teams

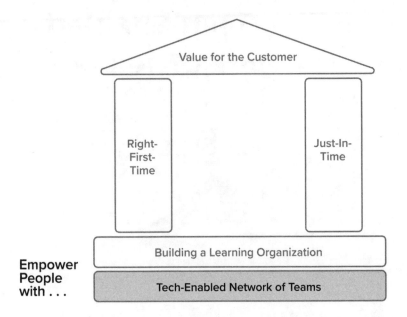

THE LINUX STORY

The Largest Software Collaboration Ever

n the summer of 1991, a Finnish programmer emailed a newsgroup:

> From: torvalds@klaava.Helsinki.FI (Linus Benedict Torvalds)
> Newsgroups: comp.os.minix
> Subject: What would you like to see most in minix?
> Summary: small poll for my new operating system
> Message-ID:
> Date: 25 Aug 91 20:57:08 GMT
> Organization: University of Helsinki
>
> Hello everybody out there using minix – I'm doing a (free)
> operating system (just a hobby, won't be big and professional
> like gnu) for 386(486) AT clones. This has been brewing
> since April, and is starting to get ready. I'd like any feedback
> on things people like/dislike in minix, as my OS resembles
> it somewhat (same physical layout of the file-system (due to
> practical reasons) among other things).

I've currently ported bash(1.08) and gcc(1.40), and things seem to work. This implies that I'll get something practical within a few months, and I'd like to know what features most people would want. Any suggestions are welcome, but I won't promise I'll implement them :-)

Linus (torvalds@kruuna.helsinki.fi)

This seemingly unimportant announcement marked the beginning of the largest software collaboration in history and, indeed, a revolution in the software industry. In 1993, just two years after the operating system had begun to take shape, over 100 developers had joined to work on Torvalds's hobby project, which eventually became the Linux operating system.[1] Thirty years into its existence, more than 55,000 people have contributed code to the operating system that now runs the top 500 supercomputers,[2] 96.3 percent of the top 1 million web servers,[3] and the vast majority of smartphones. Five billion people rely on Linux.[4]

Linux also accelerated digital transformation in the 2000s by contributing to a 100 times reduction in server costs.[5] Google, Amazon, Facebook, Netflix, Tesla, and Uber are just some of the startups that benefited from that and run on Linux. Amazon directly credits its migration from Sun to Linux, for example, for allowing it to survive the tech bubble, by helping it significantly reduce IT costs when money got tight.[6,7]

The Power of Individuals and Interactions over Processes and Tools

How did Torvalds manage to turn the product of a hobby—something he had started "just for fun"[8]—into such a transformative force? Why were the competing systems of companies such as Microsoft taken by surprise?

By leveraging the power of open-source software, Linux brought together thousands of talented individuals from all over the world and allowed them to interact over the internet to build a system that was not only free, but also better suited to their needs than the paid alternatives. As Microsoft itself admitted in leaked internal documents, "the ability of the OSS (open-source software) process to collect and harness the collective IQ of thousands of individuals across the Internet is simply amazing. More importantly, OSS evangelization scales with the size of the Internet much faster than our own evangelization efforts appear to scale."[9] This example is a great demonstration of the power of the Agile manifesto's value of "individuals and interactions over processes and tools."

The Scaling Crises of the Linux Kernel Community

But scaling to a cumulated 55,000 contributors was not without its challenges. There were in particular two major crises in its 30 years of existence, when the Linux kernel community got scared that Linus, its founder, would burn out and leave them leaderless.

Team Empowerment

The first crisis occurred around 1996. For the first five years, Torvalds had stayed in charge of checking the quality of every contribution and responded personally to contributors. But the number of contributions he received grew quickly and eventually buried him in emails.[10] It was time for him to relinquish control. The community experimented with empowering teams on different subcomponents of the kernel, which two changes made possible.

The first change was a technical innovation: the introduction of loadable kernel modules. This allowed external modules, such as a new sound card's driver, to be added "on the go," without having to entirely recompile Linux every time. (For nondevelopers, this is the equivalent of having to reinstall an operating system.) This was done for technical reasons but also had strong organizational implications. Loadable modules were technically not part of the Linux kernel anymore, which meant that the responsibility of ensuring that they worked could be delegated to module creators. This was a big weight off Torvalds's shoulders. The new architecture also turned the monolith-like kernel, which made collaboration difficult, into a modular system in which contributors could work on subsystems autonomously.

The second change was the creation of the "maintainer" role, to officialize the fact that there were now leaders in charge of supporting all the contributions to specific subsystems. The role is mostly about refereeing whether the code is good enough to be submitted to the main repository, based on a subjective evaluation of the code's "good taste."[11] When it isn't yet good enough, maintainers give feedback on how to improve it.

The combination of more modular architecture and the empowerment of maintainers and their teams allowed kernel development to be a very lightweight and decentralized process. Everyone in the world could still contribute, and Torvalds was still responsible for the final decision on whether or not to incorporate contributions into the Linux kernel. But now he could rely on the maintainers to do a first filter on contribution quality and support the contributors on what needed to be improved. These changes let the Linux community continue scaling at full speed and permitted the number of contributions to keep growing.

Tech-Enabled Networked Collaboration

But less than two years later, in 1998, the number of contributions that Torvalds had to merge into the Linux kernel became too big. The maintainers' support was no longer enough, leading to another crisis, one where the word "burnout" was used.[12] Everything stopped while Torvalds got a bit of rest before resuming his work.[13] That was not a proper solution to the problem. Frustrations around Torvalds's "dropping patches"—losing contributions—increased, reaching a head in 2002. Rob Landley, one of the many developers contributing to Linux, proposed to create a new role of "patch penguin,"[14] another name for a deputy that would take some of Torvalds's workload. Torvalds did not agree that this solution addressed the root cause of the scaling problem.

As he looked for a different type of solution, he turned to BitKeeper, a tool that some contributors used to manage source code.[15] Another Linux contributor, Larry McVow, had created BitKeeper in response to the scaling issues of 1998, building a new source code manager designed to enable distributed collaboration on large software and facilitate merging a high volume of contributions.[16] McVow had been working on BitKeeper for four years and, perhaps surprisingly for a Linux contributor, had decided to not open-source it, which had slowed down its adoption within the Linux community. McVow eventually agreed to license BitKeeper for free to Linux contributors and, despite some protests in the open-source community, Torvalds adopted it as the kernel's official source code manager.

The situation immediately improved. It transformed the previous manual patch merging, which was akin to writing a collaborative book by emailing each new contribution to Torvalds so he could piece them together manually. Now, when the contribution had been properly reviewed and didn't cause conflicts with the existing code, Torvalds just had to push a button to approve a merge. When there were conflicts between two or more contributions to the same code lines, the tool let him delegate the job of arbitrating those conflicts to maintainers. The technology transformed distributed collaboration and made it significantly easier for Torvalds to coordinate the network of teams contributing to the kernel.

When Larry McVow threatened to revoke the free BitKeeper license in 2005,[17] the technology had become so central to scaling the Linux project that Torvalds took a few weeks off to create an open-source alternative. This is how he created Git, to enable large-scale collaboration within the Linux development community. And just like when he started Linux 14 years earlier, he created a new category leader. Git is now used by 95 percent of developers globally and has allowed the number of contributions to Linux to continue scaling without any major issues since 2005.[18]

The Linux Lesson: Empower People with a Tech-Enabled Network of Teams

Linux's development is a spectacular case study of scaling a collaboration that started on the Agile value of "individuals and interactions over processes and tools." When we look at how the Linux community addressed the issues that came with scaling, two innovations stand out: the "empowered teams" organization created around maintainers and contributors in 1996, and the collaboration network enabled at scale by the modular architecture and the collaboration technologies—BitKeeper and then Git.

These innovations allow work to be distributed across a tech-enabled network of teams and recombined efficiently into a new release every two to three months. This has allowed the Linux community to scale and maintain agility.

To scale "individuals and interactions" and replicate this "tech-enabled network of teams" organization, we need to:

- Empower teams to solve problems autonomously with the support of their team leaders
- Scale collaboration with the right tech enablers

EMPOWER TEAMS
TO SOLVE PROBLEMS

Solving Problems Autonomously

An empowered team is a team with the necessary autonomy and competence to solve the problems it faces. Lean teaches us that good problem solving is an acquirable skill that everyone in the organization should master to increase their autonomy.

Deming's "Plan, Do, Check, Act"

The origins of problem solving at Toyota can be traced back to Deming's influence on industrial Japan in the 1950s. During the conferences he held for leaders of Japanese industry, he explained how he thought the scientific method could be applied to solving engineering problems by creating a four-step cycle that he called PDCA: "Plan, Do, Check, Act."

- **Plan.** Faced with a problem, what was the original expected outcome? Why didn't that happen? What are the possible countermeasures?
- **Do.** Implement the countermeasures from the previous step.

- **Check, sometimes called "Study."** Evaluate the results of the Do phase, and compare them with the expected outcome. Also evaluate what was actually done. Did anything change from the original plan?
- **Act, also called "Adjust."** Update standards to reflect what you learned in the Do and Check phases to ensure that new work builds on that information.

Teach the Plan Phase with the PISCAR

In our experience, a key aspect of teaching problem solving and PDCA is to train people on the P step: how to come up with a good plan. We have found the PISCAR framework, invented by Régis Medina and Antoine Contal,[1] to be particularly helpful for this.

PISCAR stands for:

- **Problem.** Define the problem, ideally in terms of a quantified gap from the usual expected value. Chart it on a graph that shows the evolution of the chosen value over time, with the problem marked as the moment that value departed significantly from the expectation.
- **Impact.** Assess whether solving the problem is worth the effort by describing the impact on the value for the customer.
- **Standard.** Draw the usual value flow, and then map the problem's possible causes.
- **Causes.** List at least three possible causes. Seven is ideal to stimulate out-of-the-box thinking.
- **Action.** After identifying one or more causes as most probable, plan for one or more countermeasures to address them.
- **Result (expected).** Write down the expected outcome to ensure that you later compare actual results with initial expectations. This is a key aspect of the scientific method. It reduces bias and generates validated learnings.

A PISCAR EXAMPLE

- **Problem.** Our app performance index "Apdex" (see measuring performance in "Value for the Customer") has decreased from its usual 0.8 to 0.3 since the last release. (See Figure 7.1.)

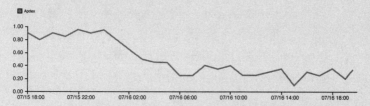

FIGURE 7.1   Evolution of an application's performance index.

- **Impact.** Low Apdex makes the app very slow for users and increases the churn.

- **Standard.** A user request usually goes through router > permission layer > controller > template.

- **Causes.** Possible causes could be:
  - ° The change to the permission system has introduced a call to a slow API (location in standard flow: permission layer).
  - ° The number of users went up significantly (location in standard flow: controller).
  - ° The number of rows in one database table has increased significantly (location in standard flow: controller).
  - ° The change in the permission system had a significant effect on the number of database requests (location in standard flow: permission layer).
  - ° A JavaScript library is slowing down rendering (location in standard flow: template).

- ◦ The hard disk of the database server is full, creating swap issues for the database (location in standard flow: permission layer + controller).
- ◦ The js code measuring Apdex has changed location in the template (location in standard flow: template).
- **Action.** Since the most probable cause is the fourth one, check in Django using the "Debug" mode whether the change in the permission layer is indeed generating multiple requests to the database. If so, try using "select_related" instead of "select."
- **(Expected) Result.** By using "select_related," the permission layer should not generate more than two requests to the database.

In this example, the custom permission layer had been modified in a way that required using a new table in the database. Because it was implemented quickly, the number of database requests had increased by an order of magnitude. But it was possible to activate a simple option in the ORM, the abstraction layer between the code and the database, to improve the situation: using "select_related" instead of "select."

This PISCAR example is an illustration of how problem solving, beyond empowering the team to solve its actual problem, is also a great learning opportunity for everyone involved. Here, those who didn't master the ORM and had never encountered the "select_related" option before could learn from teammates. More generally, thinking broadly about all the possible causes of a problem helps everyone increase their deep understanding of the technologies involved.

Train on Problem Solving

The fresh insights that a good PDCA brings to the team are the biggest arguments to convince a team to start problem solving. But while one good PDCA will create a spark, it will not be enough to make everyone on the team feel confident.

At Theodo, we have been running problem-solving dojos on a weekly basis for a very long time. During problem-solving dojos, the organization meets around one team who presents (for example) its latest PDCA on a whiteboard or shared document, inviting challenges from anyone. This is as much a training opportunity, with teams sharing ideas and best practices on how to improve problem-solving skills, as it is a collective problem-solving exercise, zooming in on the team's analysis.

The best way to learn problem solving is still through the daily support of the team leader. This means team leaders need to master problem solving, lead by example, and create accountability.

Supportive Team Leaders

The importance of supporting teams in their problem-solving efforts to empower them highlights the strategic value of a good team leader. What exactly makes a team leader good? And how can we spot good team leaders?

The Importance of Investing in Team Leaders

In *Nine Lies About Work*, Marcus Buckingham and Ashley Goodall share some of the most counterintuitive results of their management survey. The first is that "while people might care which company they join, they don't care which company they work for. The truth is that, once there, people care which team they're on."[2]

Their data is compelling. Experience at work varies more from team to team than it does from company to company. Building a culture depends more on team leaders and how they are chosen and promoted, than on any other companywide initiative.

What Is a Supportive Team Leader?

At Theodo, we try to promote supportive team leaders who are key to cultivating a strong problem-solving culture. We look for three traits in a team leader: competent, caring, and spiky.

Competent

Early on, Steve Jobs faced the dilemma of whether to hire external professional managers to manage Apple's teams of engineers. In a 1984 interview, he shared his experience:

> We went through that stage in Apple where we went out and thought, Oh, we're gonna be a big company, let's hire professional management. We went out and hired a bunch of professional management. It didn't work at all. . . . They knew how to manage, but they didn't know how to do anything. If you're a great person, why do you want to work for somebody you can't learn anything from? And you know what's interesting? You know who the best managers are? They are the great individual contributors who never, ever want to be a manager but decide they have to be . . . because no one else is going to do as good a job.[3]

If a team leader has people skills but no technical competence, then that leader will have difficulty supporting team members in their problem-solving efforts.

Competence is fairly easy to identify, especially in tech environments, where technical incompetence is hard to hide. Internal peer reviews should reveal whether a person has the competence required for a particular role.

Caring

As Simon Sinek wrote in *Leaders Eat Last*, leadership is not about being in charge. It's about taking care of those in your charge. Once people feel protected by their leaders, their natural reaction is to trust and cooperate. That in turn empowers the team to overcome difficulties and thrive together. Simon Sinek calls it the "Circle of Safety." He says, "It is easy to know when we are in the Circle of Safety because we feel it. We feel valued by our colleagues, and we feel cared for by our supervisors. We become absolutely confident that the leaders in the organization and all those with whom we work are there for us and will do what they can to help us succeed."

Determining whether someone genuinely cares about people is not easy when you are not part of the person's team. Some people, for example, might be quite absent when it comes to their team, but be sincerely sensitive to their managers' needs, leading their managers to draw the wrong conclusion.

Getting better insights into what is happening within teams is one of the reasons the leadership team should spend a lot of time on the ground. By regularly interacting with the teams and seeing what they are currently working on and how people within the teams interact, leaders can get a sense of whether people contribute to the Circle of Safety.

Spiky

The third trait we look for is spiky. It's derived from *Nine Lies About Work*, which says that what makes a good leader is not well-roundedness, but being extremely strong at one particular skill. A study by McKinsey and Egon Zhender identified something similar in 2011 and coined the word "spiky" to describe it.[4]

Spiky people make us want to follow them, regardless of their hierarchical status, because they are, in the words of Buckingham and Goodall, "deep in something, and know what that something is [which] gives us both certainty in the present and confidence in the future."

Identifying someone's "spikiness" is difficult, as people can end up in roles where they don't get to use their spike at all. This can be because leadership is not aware of the value of a certain talent, so the person keeps it quiet.

There is also a structural reason. Organizations usually start by identifying gaps and then look for people who could fill those gaps, rather than starting by identifying people's talents and thinking about where those talents could be best used. That's how organizations end up with square pegs in round holes, wasting talent and missing the potential of people who are just not where they should be.

To spot those we might have overlooked, Theodo regularly asks team members "How much, on a scale of 0 to 10, would you want to work with this Theodoer on your next project or difficult challenge?" This gives us a more bottom-up insight into who naturally inspires others, encouraging us to look further at the spike that person might possess.

Bad Team Leaders

Recognizing bad team leaders is more straightforward than identifying individuals with the right potential. Consistently low scores in bottom-up engagement surveys are a clear sign of a bad team leader.

When the leadership team sees low engagement scores or high churn in a team, it is their job to react. Collect evidence to challenge the team leader fairly and factually; then immediately train that team leader or phase the leader out of management until that leader is ready again.

Once good team leaders are identified, what is their role?

The Role of the Team Leader

Agile community members sometimes believe that self-organization is the ideal and leaders are no longer required. It is interesting to look at the point of view of Christophe Dejours, former hospital practitioner in psychiatry, psychoanalyst, and professor of the chair of Psychoanalysis, Health and Work at France's Conservatoire National des Arts et Métiers. According to Dejours, a group leader's fundamental role is to act as the referee when the group experiences a crisis. Group consensus emerges in most situations. But when it does not, the group can split into two or more disagreeing factions. The leader's role is to facilitate consensus, which might mean refereeing in favor of one option or the other. In other words, a good leader makes self-organization happen as often as possible, and acts as a referee when it doesn't, to make sure the group doesn't split.

In his book *Learning to Scale*, Régis Medina identifies six key activities on which team leaders should spend at least half their time to fulfil this role.

Visualize

To help cascade value for the customer to the team, the team leader should work on the team's visual management. This means making the team's goals, problems, and progress visible, empowering the team to react.

Support

Team leaders promptly respond to calls for help and problem-solve with team members to find and quickly implement fixes. They then take responsibility for implementing longer-term, more sustainable solutions to a problem.

Support also includes regular one-on-one meetings with team members to discuss priorities and help them succeed in their jobs. Google's "Project Oxygen" study on what makes a good manager highlighted the importance of these meetings.[5]

Escalate

The team leader escalates problems when they are too big for the team, to harness the whole organization's resources.

Train

The team leader makes sure the team is competent in its work. This means creating work standards and training material, and leveraging these in short training sessions whenever a skill gap is spotted.

Maintain

Team leaders help team members improve their working conditions to create a working environment with as few impediments and hassles as possible.

Improve

Team leaders lead daily problem-solving exercises and also engage team members in regular improvement work.

Let's dive deeper into the two aspects we feel are most often overlooked: training and maintaining.

On-the-Job Training.   In the tech industry, learning never ends. Beyond learning new languages and frameworks as the software industry evolves, mastering the crafts of good software design and good coding requires continuous learning.

Unfortunately, traditional training and development do not seem to ensure that people have the skills required to succeed. Mihnea Moldoveanu, professor at the University of Toronto's Rotman School of Management, and Das Narayandas, professor of business administration at the Harvard Business School, confirm this frustration when they estimate that barely 10 percent of the $200 billion annual investment in corporate training and development in the United States delivers concrete results.[6]

One of the reasons they highlight is the time and physical distance between when a skill is learned and when it is applied. Research in psychology and more recently in the neuroscience of learning reveals that distance greatly influences the probability that a student will put the skill into practice. To be effective, training should be held as close as possible to the situation that made the training necessary in the first place—what scientists call "near transfer."

This is why problem solving with the support of competent team leaders can be so powerful. Whenever the problem-solving exercise identifies a skill gap in a team member, the team leader can react by planning a quick one-to-one training session just a few days after noticing the gap. This minimizes the time between learning and using a skill.

Maintaining the Development Environment with 5S.   It's much easier for a team of developers to feel empowered if their development environment is an easy place to work. This is typically what a small, young organization can offer. Teams that start from scratch, called "greenfield" in software, know exactly where to find what they are looking for and where to add their new contributions, whether in the codebase, the deployment pipeline, or the production infrastructure.

In larger and older organizations, however, teams have to work within existing systems and typically depend on other teams and past contributions. For every contribution they try to make, they must take into account what already exists and how their contribution might break the existing systems. Without enough investment in keeping the development environment "clean," understanding how and where to contribute can require hours of reading through difficult code and talking to other teams. It can end up taking much more time than the contribution itself. This reduces the team's autonomy and is very disempowering.

Lean thinking uses a method called "5S" to help a team maintain the clarity of its working environment. The team leader's role is to help the team members agree on what clarity looks like for them and what regular efforts are needed to maintain it. The name "5S" comes from the five steps of workplace organization the method describes, the words for which all start with an *S* in Japanese: *Seiri, Seiton, Seiso, Seiketsu,* and *Shitsuke.*

The most common English translation retains the initial *S*: sort, set in order, shine, standardize, and sustain. This translation alliterates nicely, but unfortunately does not indicate what each step is actually about. Our translation would be:

- Delete what's no longer used.
- Sort and label what's left.
- Clean everything back to an "almost new" state, to identify the issues the messiness is hiding.
- Create a system to regularly maintain the previous three steps.
- Get leadership to sponsor and support the system.

Here are three examples of 5S applied to our tech working environments.

5S on a Continuous Integration/Continuous Deployment Pipeline

For a continuous integration pipeline, which can take more and more time to execute if left unattended, regular 5S can be:

- Delete useless tests and unused fixtures.
- Sort and label the test suites.
- Clean the "false negatives" away.
- Invent a system and a routine to maintain clean tests—for example, practicing test-driven development as a team.
- Get leadership's support on testing, for example, by investing in a testing infrastructure to make tests run faster.

5S on Production Monitoring

For production monitoring, which can end up producing more noise than signal if left unattended, regular 5S could be:

- Delete useless alerts.
- Sort and label (with tags, for example) the remaining alerts.
- Address all the ongoing alerts, to reach 0 open alerts.
- Invent a system and routine to make the three previous steps happen continuously. For example, devise a weekly routine to address all the nonurgent alerts that could typically be ignored for weeks, and get to the root cause of every alert to ensure the problem will not return.
- Get leadership to sponsor these 5S efforts, for example, by buying large screens to display the monitoring in the open space.

5S in a Codebase

In the software world, two similar approaches have already popularized the idea of maintaining a codebase to make it easier to work with: Robert Martin's clean code and Martin Fowler's refactoring. One of Robert Martin's strong arguments for maintaining code readability is the time spent reading it. "The ratio of time spent reading versus writing is well over 10 to 1. We are constantly reading old code as part of the effort to write new code,"he writes.[7]

The 5S version of maintaining a clean codebase could be:

- Identify and delete unused code.
- Label parts of the code that are hard to understand or are regular sources of defects, using a tool like Tyrion.[8]
- In parts that need immediate action, move files to the right folders, classes to the right files, and functions to the right classes. Rename them with explicit labeling.
- Create routines determining when and how to apply 5S to the codebase. For example, Martin Fowler's routine is "Always leave the code base healthier than when you found it. It will never be perfect, but it should be better."[9]
- Finally, get leadership to sponsor efforts to refactor code regularly. That's where the example of the Linux maintainers is most telling: by only merging code that follows "good taste," they sustain high standards.

An important warning about maintaining code: when introducing a change in a working codebase, there is always a trade-off between improving its readability and potentially introducing a defect. That trade-off needs to be weighed carefully and countermeasures implemented to reduce the possible side effects. For example, have a thorough cover of automated tests or enforce pair programming on such tasks.

These examples can be used as starting points. 5S is powerful only if every team is empowered to come up with its own approach. As Michael

Ballé says in an article about this method, "5S is not about creating the perfect workspace on paper and implementing it. It's a self-study and self-development method for the team to come together on having things exactly as they want them, where they want them."[10] 5S efforts should come from the team, facilitated and supported by the team leader.

Focusing on how team leaders support the team leads to another question: How does the leadership team support the team leaders?

A Supportive Leadership Team

Gemba walks are the perfect time for the leadership team to show support for the team leaders and their teams. They're an opportunity to both show a deep interest in a team's problem-solving activities and consider what the observed issues mean for the overall business strategy.

Gemba walks are also an opportunity to provide concrete support, whether it's by getting directly involved in a problem-solving initiative or unblocking some resources to tackle a basic problem.

These walks can help managers better understand the bigger patterns of what prevents teams on the ground from creating value and addressing these patterns to ensure the teams stay empowered.

One recurring problem that would appear quickly on the topic of empowering teams is the challenge of maintaining team autonomy at scale when teams depend on more and more external systems and other teams. This is where we must leverage the right technologies to scale collaboration without reducing autonomy.

SCALE COLLABORATION WITH THE RIGHT TECH ENABLERS

Technology, a Double-Edged Sword

Technology is a double-edged sword. When it is well designed and functional, it can be a formidable enabler, increasing individual productivity and facilitating collaboration between people. However, when it doesn't work as expected, such as intermittent Wi-Fi, a broken laptop, or buggy software, technology can make working conditions terrible, distract a team from doing its job, and turn collaboration into a burden.

How can we make sure we leverage the enabling opportunity while minimizing the friction?

Enable Networked Collaboration

Technology can be a formidable enabler of collaboration as we have seen in the Linux kernel example, where BitKeeper and then Git solved the bottleneck of merging the contributions of the different teams, making it much easier for teams to work together in a distributed way. Another powerful illustration is what happened at Amazon around 2002.

Amazon's API Mandate

In 2002, Amazon.com was still a big monolith, both in the codebase and in its organization. In *Working Backwards*, Colin Bryar, who had joined four years earlier, shares his experience as technical product manager in the Amazon Associates Program. This was the product that allowed any website to place links to Amazon products and get a cut, a referral fee, if the visitor it had sent to Amazon ended up buying the product. This is now called "affiliate marketing" and is a huge customer acquisition channel on the internet, but at the time it was still quite new and no one was sure how big it could become.

Bryar's first task was to extend the referral fee not just to the product the website had linked to, but to any product bought by the customer that the website had kindly redirected to Amazon. Since customers would often end up on Amazon thanks to the link but buy different products, it seemed fair to compensate for the other products, too. Bryar estimated that would be an easy technical task, where most of the work would be in updating the reporting, accounting, and payment systems to take into account that change.

That's when he discovered how difficult it had become to make changes to the Amazon website. All the code resided in one large executable program to which every team contributed. Any change, even a small one, affected many other teams, so avoiding bugs required a lot of coordination.

The database was an even more challenging dependency. Since all of Amazon relied on a single database, any mistake could cause the website to go down for hours. Every change had to be reviewed and approved jointly by the CTO, the head of database administration, and the head of data. Since they met only a few times each month, a change to the database could take weeks or months to be approved and implemented.

The outcome was that on everything Bryar's team controlled—accounting, reporting, and payment—work was finished quickly, even though these things made up the bulk of the team's effort. Meanwhile, the minor changes that the team needed to make to other teams' code and to the central database ended up taking months, waiting painfully for the necessary coordination meetings and database reviews to happen.

Bryar's team was not the only one facing this issue. The slow coordination meant that only a few big projects could be delivered each quarter, way fewer than the number of good business ideas that Amazon teams had. Trying to decide which ones to pursue and ensure that scarce resources went to the most impactful initiatives, Amazon came up with a first solution: a centralized process called New Project Initiatives (NPI) that would help the organization communicate and coordinate around priorities. Every quarter, every project that required resources from other teams (in practice, this was most projects) would submit an application to be considered a global priority. Applications that passed the first screening would then be reviewed in a very large and long meeting, and the projects that made it through the whole process would then move forward relatively quickly.

This approach seemed the best solution to coordinate all the dependencies, but it was disheartening to everyone involved. It took a long time to prepare for the meeting, too many projects didn't make the cut, and those that did were often approved based on wrong assumptions, as it was very difficult to estimate early on how successful the project would be and how long it would take.

By planning everything up front in a centralized, top-down, and faceless process, NPI embodied the opposite of Agile. Everyone dreaded it. No one wanted to be on one of the many teams whose projects hadn't made the cut and who would be reassigned to support other teams. This was not only bad for morale; it also went against Amazon's culture of creating an environment in which talent had maximum latitude to invent and build things to delight customers.

That's when Jeff Bezos had an aha moment. "For Amazon to be a place where builders can build, we need to eliminate communication, not encourage it." He proposed that instead of looking for new ways to better manage dependencies, Amazon should find a way to remove them by reorganizing the engineering organization into smaller teams that would be autonomous, connected to other teams only loosely and only when unavoidable. That way the teams would be able to do their work in parallel and spend less time coordinating and more time building.

To make that happen would require a gigantic shift in the IT organization and a lot of hard work before reaping the benefits. The task went to someone who was not afraid of a tough challenge: Rick Dalzell, a West Point graduate who had served seven years in the U.S. Army. Dalzell collected inputs from across the company on how to achieve Bezos's vision and came back with a model to transform the organization into a network of hundreds of two-pizza teams, a name coined to describe teams that could be fed with just two pizzas. Some of the characteristics envisaged for these teams were:

- No more than 10 people.
- They would own everything from business to design to technology.
- Clear metrics for evaluating their work, monitored in real time.
- Technically autonomous, thanks to APIs.

Once the model was agreed, Dalzell started the transformation. One of the hardest parts of that plan was making the teams technically autonomous. It required migrating the Amazon monolith to a service architecture and then requiring all the teams to use the interfaces provided by those services, rather than accessing the database directly as they once had.[1]

In software engineering, service interfaces are called "application programming interfaces," or APIs, and this is why this transformation became known as "the API mandate."[2] The first two-pizza teams had to invest months of work up front to create the right APIs and eliminate the technical dependencies. But once the teams were able to use other teams' services without the need for coordination, they could innovate and deliver results at full speed, just like in the early days of Amazon.

By defining communication across teams as a "defect," Jeff Bezos reframed the problem completely and justified the need to migrate to a new architecture. The hard work Rick Dalzell and Amazon's engineering teams performed in creating APIs everywhere reduced cross-team dependencies and paid off by reenabling agility in the teams, a key factor in Amazon's hypergrowth from $4 billion revenue in 2002 to more than $500 billion in 2022.

It also contributed directly to that top-line growth by creating the premises for Amazon's cloud revolution. Once that transformation had demonstrated that even infrastructure could be provided as a service through an API—an idea no one seemed to have had before, despite the fact that most tech businesses needed this product—the urge to service these new customers became overwhelming. Amazon launched its first cloud product in late 2004, followed by two more in 2006, including on-demand servers with "Elastic Compute Cloud." Eighteen years later, cloud services represented $80 billion in company revenue.[3]

Tesla's Software-Defined Vehicle

Many leading tech companies have now embraced the idea of making teams more autonomous using APIs, and not just in the software. Tesla's car design follows the principles of "modular architecture" and "contract-first design" from extreme manufacturing.[4]

Tesla used these principles to make car design more modular and allow teams to contribute more autonomously. It also innovated in combining these modules together using software rather than the traditional electronic control units used by the rest of the industry.

This abstraction of the underlying modules and hardware, also known as "software-defined vehicle architecture," allows a much better decoupling of the different parts of the car and therefore faster iterations of each module.[5]

Eliminate Communication

APIs are communication contracts in a modular architecture. They allow each module to evolve autonomously while preserving, by sticking to the contract, the communication ability with other modules. That's why they scale the organization not by improving coordination, but by eliminating the need for coordination once the contract is agreed and maintained.

The trade-off is that the contract needs to be upheld. As the APIs become critical in an IT architecture and replace in many places what used to be database calls, they need to become as reliable as a database. That is why in the legend surrounding Bezos's API mandate he asked that all service interfaces be designed from the ground up to be externalizable. In line with Cagan's "platform teams," the goal of this directive is to ensure that teams exposing critical APIs realize they need to make them as reliable to their internal customers within the organization as the kind of service level agreements they would guarantee to an external customer.

Modular architectures and APIs are a technological solution to an organizational problem, by eliminating communication in many areas. But what about the situations where work needs to be merged and eliminating communication is not possible?

Collaboration Enablers

Where communication is still needed, technology can also act as a powerful enabler by reducing friction and conflicts.

Coordinating multiple people who are working on the same document used to be very difficult, whether the document was text, code, design, or a movie. Initially, even Linux had this problem. Each contributor's work was manually merged by Linus Torvalds, who had to check whether two people had worked on the same lines of code, and when that happened, either decide himself how to deal with conflicting changes or ask the contributors to find an agreement. In coding, these issues are very common and are called "merge conflicts." When the Linux community reached a certain size, it became impossible for Torvalds to deal with all these merges by himself. Yet he refused to believe that this problem couldn't be effectively tackled with technology, and indeed as we have seen, the adoption of BitKeeper in 2002 and of Git in 2005 proved him right. Thanks to an ingenious approach to distributed collaboration, Git drastically reduces the number of merge conflicts, allows contributors to better deal with merges in a decentralized manner, and makes the remaining conflicts much easier to handle. This all made it possible for Torvalds to continue acting as chief architect on all merges, while the community around him grew by another order of magnitude.

Technology that makes collaboration much easier has now spread to every domain. Online SaaS (software as service) solutions have done so in collaborative writing, for example, with tools like Google Docs, Microsoft Word 365, or Notion, or in collaborative design with tools such as Adobe Creative Cloud, Canva, or Figma. Such technologies enable people to work online on the same document and see each other's changes in real time, eliminating all the conflicts that existed before when synchronization was not instantaneous.

Network of Teams

By combining technology that eliminates much of the need for communication with technology that reduces friction when communication is needed, we are able to distribute work across a large number of teams. This allows the teams to work autonomously and recombine their contributions easily, and it effectively turns the organization into a network of teams. When an organization is able to do it at scale, it creates a multiplier force that makes it very hard for competitors to catch up, as Linux demonstrated when it replaced Microsoft and Sun on the server market.

The challenge, however, is that this creates an even bigger reliance on technology. How can we make sure that those technologies work reliably?

Enable Friction-Free Working Conditions

Rely on Commodity Hardware

Those who were at Theodo 10 years ago remember fondly when everyone in the company was autonomous in choosing their computers. But at the time this meant spending the first days building your own desktop PC, and we don't look back with nostalgia at the regular hardware issues that would ensue, from requiring careful inspection of what went wrong to ordering the new parts. Not only did we have to wait a long time for the new parts to arrive, but nontechnical team members were reliant on their more expert colleagues to help them.

Faced with that challenge at a much larger scale, Google's initial solution was to establish a loaner laptop program so that whenever people had an issue, they could just borrow a laptop from the IT help desk. But this still took time, required paperwork, and required a lot of work from the IT staff.

Not satisfied with that situation, Google went a step further in 2016 and launched the "grab-and-go" program, a self-service shelf stacked with Chromebooks that anyone at Google can just take. And by signing into their account, Googlers get instant access to all their usual software and information, thanks to the cloud.

As a result, Googlers are now autonomous. They just take a laptop whenever they have an issue and put it back in the rack when they're done. After just a year, the grab-and-go racks around Google's offices had enabled more than 100,000 loans, saving tens of thousands of hours to the users and the IT help desk staff.[6]

You don't need to be Google anymore to have this commoditized approach to hardware and software and give employees autonomous access to reliable technology. With high-quality laptops now readily available and by moving everything to the cloud, any computer can act as a temporary replacement. A simple trip to the nearest store is enough to buy a new machine and makes team members as autonomous with their hardware at work as they are at home.

Implement Autonomous Mini-Audits with the Kamishibai Approach

The commoditized approach to hardware and software cannot be applied to every system in the organization. One example is videoconferencing systems in meeting rooms, where the hardware is not readily available and for which no one feels really responsible. Another is any backup system that was installed a while ago, but needs regular testing if it is to work the day it is actually needed.

Lean thinking gives us an interesting approach to address these kinds of issues while maintaining as much team autonomy as possible: mini-audits supported by a visual management tool that empowers self-service, known as the *kamishibai* board.

The name "kamishibai" is inspired by a traditional form of Japanese street theater, typically meant for children, that uses picture cards for storytelling. The board contains one card for each type of issue that we want regular audits to prevent. Anyone in the organization can pick up a card, read about the issue this card aims to prevent, understand the importance of the associated audit, and feel compelled to go do it. Once the audit is done, the card goes back to the board on the green side if everything was fine and on the red side if the audit found a problem that requires corrective action.

Here are a few examples of maintenance problems that can benefit from a kamishibai approach:

- Regularly checking that the videoconferencing systems work in every meeting room
- Rebuilding the development environment from scratch on a regular basis, to ensure it is well automated
- Launching a fresh rebuild of the production infrastructure from the backups, to test both the quality of the "infrastructure as code" automation and the backup systems

This approach lets an organization tackle maintenance while keeping the teams as autonomous as they can be.

Scaling Autonomy with Technology

Toyota, Amazon, Google, Tesla, and other successful tech leaders have built their organizations on networks of teams. This allows them to maintain the benefits of the Agile value of "individuals and interactions over processes and tools" within the teams, while scaling the number of teams.

To help teams stay empowered, we coach them on problem solving, with the support of team leaders and regular go and sees from the organizational leadership. This creates the right conditions to combine psychological safety with motivation and accountability and help teams perform.

To maintain teams' autonomy at scale, we leverage technology to reduce dependencies and friction and distribute work better, allowing the organization to collaborate without the need for endless coordination meetings.

This "tech-enabled network of teams," empowered on value for the customer, creates a solid foundation for an Agile organization. Let's now look at how to leverage that agility to help the organization produce high-quality products with right-first-time.

PART FOUR

Produce Higher Quality with Right-First-Time

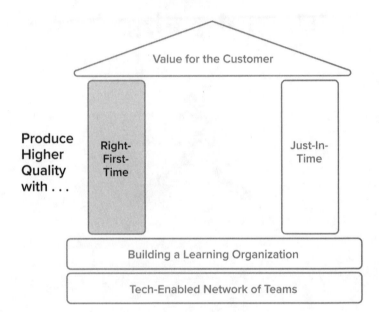

THE THERAC-25
BUGS STORY

After the success of its Therac-6 and Therac-20 radiation therapy machines, Atomic Energy of Canada Limited (AECL) decided to manufacture a new, more automated version of its product: the Therac-25. Radiation therapy machines send high-energy beams of electrons or x-rays toward a patient's tumor to try to kill the cancerous cells and cause as little collateral damage as possible to the healthy tissue around them. The Therac machines offer both electrons and x-rays so the doctors can choose the best beam depending on the patient's needs. In the first models, a radiotherapy technician could switch between the two modes automatically or manually. The goal of the Therac-25 was to remove the manual option so the switching could happen faster, wasting less time and treating more patients. The new design was released in 1983, building on top of the Therac-6 and Therac-20.

For two years, the Therac-25 treated thousands of patients with no mistakes reported. In 1985, however, a machine malfunction burned a patient, who lost her left breast and left arm. That same year, two more patients were burned. One would have needed a complete hip replacement if she hadn't died from her cancer, while the other required a skin graft to close the wounds caused by excessive radiation.

After each incident, the local hospital's physicist called AECL and the medical regulation bureau to investigate. Each time, AECL carefully ran test after test, but was never able to reproduce the error. Desperately looking for a cause, it blamed a hardware failure and changed the microswitches on all the machines. Yet, the following year, two more patients suffered radiation overdoses and died.

It took the strong-willed Fritz Hager, a staff physicist at the East Texas Cancer Center in Tyler, Texas, where the two deaths had occurred, to finally properly dig into the issue on his own initiative. Realizing that the same radiotherapy technician had been involved in both incidents, Hager brought her in to try and re-create the problem. After a couple of days of investigation, the two were finally able to identify the issue. Setting up the machine for high-powered x-rays took about eight seconds, but if the user switched to electron mode within that time frame, the software would not take the change into account and the turntable wouldn't move to the right position, thus creating a dangerous situation. The root cause of the problem was not a rare hardware issue, but a repeatable software bug, triggered when operating the machine in a very specific way. The company finally analyzed the software in detail and identified multiple bugs—unfortunately, not before another patient died.

These bugs had escaped scrutiny because they had never been triggered during the Therac manufacturer's extensive and repeated end-to-end testing efforts. In her thorough analysis of the Therac-25 incidents,[1] Nancy Leveson, an American specialist in system and software safety, determined that the "working software" reused from the previous models was actually low quality for such a critical system. There were few comments, no tests, and, indeed, more than one bug. These bugs had evaded the multiple tests for two reasons: in the older versions of the machine, a software bug would prompt a hardware fuse to blow, preventing any incidents from occurring. Sadly, the fuse had been removed from the Therac-25. And the bugs were race conditions and overflows that were triggered in the kind of edge cases that only a busy human operator can come up with, but never appeared in the rational scenarios that the extensive system testing had repeated.

For Nancy Leveson, extensive system testing to determine whether the software is working was not a good enough quality approach, considering the life-threatening impact it could have. To prevent the defects that no amount of final testing could detect, building a complex system like the Therac-25 required fostering a high-quality culture throughout its development process, in particular:

- **Defensive design.** The Therac-25 software did not contain self-checks or other error-detection features that would have detected the inconsistencies and coding errors earlier.
- **Elimination of root causes.** Patching only the symptoms and ignoring the deeper underlying causes were unlikely to have much effect on future accidents.
- **Safer design to prevent mistakes.** Both the software design and the user interface made mistakes likely. For example, there was no separation between the code handling the keyboard and the code handling the radiotherapy. Everything was written in assembly code, a machine language very hard for human beings to read and understand.

Only a built-in-quality approach would have ensured that real-life usage, which diverts from testing scenarios, didn't end up causing accidents.

Aiming for Right-First-Time to Achieve Built-in Quality

The Therac-25 story and Nancy Leveson's analysis show us that when code is critical, whether that's because it's deployed to more people or because recipients rely on it for critical uses, "working software" is not enough. To produce the higher quality required, we need to strive for the right-first-time ideal:

- Adopt a jidoka approach of detecting and stopping at defects as early as possible to demonstrate that quality is not a pick-and-choose activity, but an integral part of the work.
- Adopt a dantotsu approach of systematically analyzing the defects to learn from them and exterminate their root causes.
- Create poka-yokes: mistake-preventing environments to avoid mindless mistakes whenever possible.

人10

JIDOKA: DETECT AND STOP AT DEFECTS EARLY

The Origin of Jidoka

Jidoka's origin story goes back to 1897, when Sakichi Toyoda, Toyota's founder, was trying to improve automatic looms. He realized that looms had operators—often children, whose labor was cheap—who watched the machines nonstop to detect the moment a warp thread broke. They then stopped the looms or tried to repair the thread while the machine was running, one of the many sources of accidents that could result in lost fingers.

To remedy this problem, Toyoda invented a warp-halting device, a mechanism that stopped the loom as soon as one of the threads broke. This reduced accidents, reduced quality defects by stopping the machine before the fabric was damaged,[1] and also increased productivity by letting the operators move freely from one machine to another, rather than stay at a single loom to detect defects.

Andon Systems

To implement a similar approach, we need to find ways to automatically detect defects as early as possible and immediately tell the team in charge. This is what the Toyota Production System calls an *Andon*. In Japanese, an Andon is a paper lantern. Toyota used the word to refer to automated yellow and red lights that appear wherever quality issues are detected. The red lights show the team leader where to go to help a team member tackle the situation.

The Andon cord that inspired Jeff Bezos to create "the big red button" is not the only type of Andon. There are actually two types:

- Andon systems where a process or automated check finds defects and triggers the warning lamp automatically
- The Andon cord[2] that anyone in the company can pull to stop production and summon the team leader

The romanticized image of employees pulling the Andon cord to stop the production line should not make us forget that this should be the fallback option when automatic defect detection isn't possible.

In the typical software development life cycle, there are multiple stages where implementing early defect detection Andon systems is possible. As mentioned in Part Two, identifying detection stages and then categorizing defects by when they were detected helps measure progress and creates an incentive to catch more of them earlier. As a reminder, here are the stages we came up with for software development:

- **A** if the defect was detected by the developer in a final review, before pushing the code
- **B** if it was detected by someone else on the team or by the continuous integration pipeline before reaching an internal customer
- **C** if it was detected after reaching an internal customer (product owner, QA, etc.) and before pushing to production

- **D** if it was detected after pushing to production, where it could have affected an external customer, and before receiving a complaint
- **E** if it resulted in a customer complaint

Let's see how these different stages play out in a software environment.

Stage A—Detected Before Push by the Developer

Auto-quality is the key in achieving superior quality. We have seen more than one Q&A team, newly created to improve quality, actually let the rest of the organization outsource quality checks and disengage with their own quality efforts. Not only did the number of defects not decrease much, but productivity dropped and delays increased because the Q&A team was busy with all the quality issues that should have been caught much earlier.

Defects are not accidental; they are produced. Jidoka empowers a defect's producer to detect it. This is what auto-quality is about: improving quality at the place where defects happen. At Theodo, in the teams where developers have adopted the discipline of counting the "A defects," we have defined them as any defect caught during their final self-inspection, just before pushing the code to the shared repository. If the self-check surfaces any issue that requires some additional rework, then that piece of work loses the "right-first-time" label and the developer flags an A defect.

Our experience is that teams that count A defects engage strongly in auto-quality and quickly adopt test-driven development as a way to increase the amount of right-first-time work.

Stage B—Detected Before Reaching an Internal Customer: Code Reviews and Continuous Integration

The second stage of defect detection is before publishing the code outside the team. This can typically be through peer code reviews within the team or continuous integration pipelines.

Code Reviews

Code reviews are an opportunity to detect quality issues that are not just defects, but also design choices that could have a negative effect on the overall quality.

This includes variable or function names that make the code difficult for future developers to understand. Making sure the code is very easy to read is an important aspect of code quality.

Code reviews can also spot short-termist architecture decisions: code that fits current product requirements too tightly and will make it difficult to adapt to future ones. Finding the right balance between not overinvesting in an uncertain future and not overfitting to short-term requirements is the kind of trade-off where a second opinion from the code review can be valuable.

Continuous Integration Pipelines

Continuous integration is another Stage B defect detection system. At first, continuous integration was the practice of merging all developers' working copies to a shared mainline several times a day. Today it refers to not only merging the code, but also running automated tests on the merged code.

These automated tests usually include the small unit tests that developers create while coding, as well as more time-consuming automated tests, such as end-to-end tests that simulate a user going through predefined journeys within the product. These tests are great at detecting regressions: defects resulting from changes made by one developer that have broken something that once worked somewhere else in the system.

Automated testing has become standard in software but can also be found in other industries. With his software background, Elon Musk brought continuous integration to Tesla's manufacturing. Seeing that the tests at the end of the car production line required for homologation were manual, he pushed for the creation of self-driving capabilities that would let every single car put itself through automated nondestructive compliance and certification tests. This is called "Factory Mode" and inspired the Autopilot capability.

Stage C—Detected Before Pushing to Production: Functional Reviews

Although the development teams should not rely on others to check their work, they need people outside the development teams, with a lot of empathy for product users, to perform final checks on whether the functionality actually behaves in the way a user would expect. For example, this helps discover defects that the development teams may have missed because they didn't understand the user well enough to identify all edge cases. It is also the step where we typically discover product defects: design or content choices that the target user will find confusing and that should be corrected.

Stage D—Detected After Pushing in Production but Before Receiving a Complaint: Continuous Deployment and Monitoring

Once technical and product checks cannot find any more defects, the next step is to ship the product to users. However, this does not mean that we stop defect detection. On the contrary, shipping actually lets us automate quality checks closer and closer to the real world, with techniques such as canary deployment and smoke testing.

Canary Deployment

When Facebook moved to continuous deployment in 2017, it designed the pipeline to make the deployment progressive. After running a final set of automated tests, the pipeline deploys an updated version that is only visible to Facebook employees. Some employees use Facebook.com during their working hours (we assume it's allowed at Facebook!), and others use the site in their leisure time, which lets the system detect issues that were not caught by automated testing. After a while, if no Facebook employee has pushed the emergency stop button, the updates are further deployed to 2 percent of customers. Bit by bit, if the monitoring systems don't catch any issues, updates are finally rolled out to all users.[3]

This is a typical example of canary deployment: rolling out the update to a small subset of users first, to detect edge cases that can be found only in production and prevent them from reaching everyone.

Smoke Testing

Smoke testing consists of doing a systematic, automated health check once a change is live. The idea is to regularly run a set of end-to-end tests on the live product, to ensure that critical behaviors are still working as expected.

Monitoring

When the tests detect no defects in the change, it is not time to lower your guard. Some defects are so subtle or complex that they only become visible much later, after the system is in use for a while. Monitoring's role is to detect these defects. This set of sensors permanently runs on the app and infrastructure to detect any unexpected behaviors. This helps identify defects faster than end users and provides technical context around problems, something end users can rarely do.

In the Therac example, if monitoring had been in place, it would have spotted software bugs in the earlier Therac-6 and Therac-20 models. The manufacturer could have corrected these before they reached the Therac-25 design, where they harmed patients.

Stage E—Detected by a User

This is the stage we absolutely want to avoid: defects that have reached the users and have only been detected after some of them complained to the customer service. Take these customer complaints seriously. For each customer complaining, there are probably a dozen who faced the same issue but couldn't be bothered to get in touch. Quickly communicate the issues they raise to the product team for correction, as these are the most costly defects.

Jidoka aims to prevent defects from reaching the users by detecting them as early as possible and stopping to fix them right away. Another benefit of early detection is that it also reduces the impact on the organization and the cost of fixing them.

But producing higher quality cannot just rely on fixing defects early. We also need to learn how to prevent them from being produced in the future.

11

DANTOTSU: LEARN FROM SYSTEMATIC DEFECT ANALYSIS

adao Nomura had been at Toyota Motor Corporation since 1965 when he was asked to help improve quality at Toyota Logistics & Forklift in 2006. It was not his first time leading quality improvements programs. He had successfully turned around a GM plant in Australia and then helped Toyota South Africa achieve the quality levels Toyota HQ needed in order to authorize global export.

He had done all this from the inside, building strong relationships with teams over many years. This time he was asked to do it as an advisor for seven plants, the majority of which were recently acquired, across five countries. He started the typical Lean way, with many go and see visits on the Gemba. He shared his problem-solving insights with management. But no real change happened. It seemed no one was really paying attention to his advice. The fact that the plants' quality had been considered good before Toyota bought them didn't help. Nomura tried twice more to share his wisdom, without success.

After the third attempt had failed and a year had passed, he changed strategy to make sure quality would become a priority. With support from headquarters, he created a program that he called "Dantotsu Quality Activities." *Dantotsu* is a Japanese term that means "extreme," "radical," or "unparalleled." The program was based on recognizing the need to improve quality and getting everyone to agree to the ambitious goal of halving defects every year for three years, for a three-year target of 88 percent defect reduction.

By creating this huge, clear focus on quality improvement, he finally brought change to the factories. Teams on the ground had seen previous quality programs fail before, so they only half-trusted the new one. But they also realized the need for something different, and Nomura was definitely bringing that.

For those who couldn't believe such ambitious targets were achievable, he started organizing visits to Japan four times a year to let them see firsthand what "good" looked like. Leveraging his experience, he helped the teams in the different factories install a set of practices to embed quality in their work. After eight years, the seven plants had reduced defects by between 91 and 98 percent. Raymond Corporation, the U.S. plant, won the "Best Plant Award" from *Industry Week* magazine as a result.

Nomura shares his story in his book *The Toyota Way of Dantotsu Radical Quality Improvement*. Although it is about improving quality in manufacturing plants, it has been a huge source of inspiration for us in adopting a right-first-time approach in software engineering. It's there that we found the inspiration to measure defects not by priority levels but by detection stages.

Another key practice we took from dantotsu is the systematic analysis of defects by the team where the defect was produced. This helps the team learn very quickly where the quality issues come from and how to prevent them.

Andons and the Chain of Help

Competence, not motivation, is the first obstacle to a culture of fixing defects and learning from them. Nothing is more frustrating and stressful than spending time on a defect without knowing how to correct it or why it happened. All the while, you feel the pressure of the clock ticking and know the organization is wondering why nothing is changing.

That's when the Andon cord comes into play and why the team leader has a key role. The team leader must create a culture where a struggling developer feels comfortable pulling the Andon cord and asking for help. To create that culture, team leaders must consistently spend time on the following habits:

- Be very reactive to an Andon call. Respond in minutes, not hours or days. Team leaders must be readily available.
- Be helpful. Team leaders must be as competent as possible. Trigger the Andon chain all the way to the top of the organization, until the answer is found.
- Be supportive and positive when discovering simple misconceptions or symptoms of mindlessness. Team leaders must be caring and have a growth mindset.

A high number of pulls on the Andon cord is an indication of good-quality team leaders. The more available, helpful, and caring they are, the more their teams will find it natural to ask for help when they are struggling.

Learning from the Defect

Once the competence gap is addressed, it is still not easy to agree on the root cause of a defect. We have seen quite a few arguments where one side argues that the root cause is a missing test, while the other side argues that a missing test is not a root cause and that we should rather look for a developer's misconception as the defect's cause. Dantotsu settles the debate by saying that we should look at both sides every time. And yes, this means doing two separate analyses every time.

The first analysis is of how the team could have detected the defect at an earlier stage. This can produce insights on ways to improve the detection mechanism, whether it's by adding some monitoring or a test, improving the test data, or adding a rule to the linter, the automated checks running in the background.

The second analysis is of how the team could have avoided the defect. We do this by asking "Why?" until we identify the misconception a developer relied on, leading to the defect. Some examples of misconceptions can be a skills gap ("We didn't know that the PopperJS library required a modifier prop"), a naming issue ("We assumed that the 'getAllProducts' function returned all products, not just the available ones"), or a domain misconception ("We didn't realize that accountants always expected to see the price without VAT first"). (See Figure 11.1.)

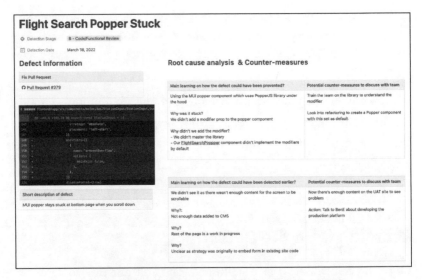

FIGURE 11.1   Example of a dantotsu defect analysis.

Checking for Other Occurrences of That Defect

Once the defect is better understood, it's key to look for all other occurrences in the code and fix them. This important step can actually yield short-term quality improvements by detecting dormant bugs before they announce themselves.

There is no automatic way to do this. The only advice we can give is to train on regular expression skills to get confident about searching patterns in a large codebase.

Sharing the Learnings and Potential Countermeasures

Understanding the root causes of the defect will lead to ideas of countermeasures, changes to the system that will reduce the occurrence of that defect. But in front of a complex system, the team should not rush to implement those countermeasures. Reacting to every defect could introduce more instability than actual improvement.

The priority should be to share the learnings with the rest of the team to improve everyone's mastery of the system. And only then implement a selection of countermeasures every week from among those the team found most sensible upon further reflection.

The best countermeasures are changes to the system that will make it impossible in the future for developers to introduce similar defects. Let's look at the different ways to achieve that in software.

12

POKA-YOKE: CREATE MISTAKE-PREVENTING ENVIRONMENTS

Systems that make mistakes impossible are known as poka-yoke in Lean thinking. They are actually fairly common in daily life. Most of the electrical plugs we use, for example, have poka-yoke built into them. They are designed so that you cannot insert a plug in a way that would cause damage. This might be because there is no wrong way, as in the USB-C design, or because it's impossible to plug it the wrong way, as in the USB-A design.

The failed launch of the European Arianespace Vega rocket in November 2020 is an example of what a lack of poka-yoke can produce. Two cables involved in the thrust vector control system were incorrectly connected during assembly. Roland Lagier, Arianespace's chief technical officer, blamed a human error.[1] Designing these cables to make that human error impossible would have been a poka-yoke.

In software, initial system designs and tooling choices can prevent mistakes and have a strong effect on the resulting quality. For example, a study by Microsoft research[2] showed that using TypeScript or Flow instead of JavaScript could prevent 15 percent of the bugs observed in JavaScript code, thanks to static-type systems that detect type errors automatically. Another study by Veracode observed that 59 percent of the C++ applications studied had severe or very severe flaws, compared with just 24 percent in Java, where automatic memory management prevents many of the errors observed in C++ code.[3]

Technical leadership can therefore help prevent mistakes with the right tech strategy. Let's look at some of the choices available.

Choosing Languages That Prevent Mistakes

As mentioned, some languages make it harder to introduce coding bugs. The features that facilitate quality in a programming language include:

- **Static-type checking.**[4] Static typing is a way for a programmer to restrict the kind of data that can be stored in a variable—for example, defining that the variable "age" can only be a number, while the variable "siblings" is a list, potentially empty, containing people. Static typing is a good example of poka-yoke. The language won't let the developer write "age = 'John'". This is why, in the study mentioned before, 15 percent of the bugs typically found in JavaScript code were instantly detected by TypeScript or Flow.
- **Null safety.**[5] Tony Hoare, the computer scientist who first introduced the idea that all variables could have a null value in a new programming language he was designing, now calls this design decision his "billion-dollar mistake."[6] Many object-oriented languages were influenced by his design and don't prevent the manipulation of null objects. This lets developers write code that will work if the object exists, but will crash as soon as the manipulated object turns out to be null. The languages that don't let this happen are called "null-safe languages." Recent object-oriented languages that implement null safety by default are Kotlin, Rust, Dart, and

Swift. Others can also implement null safety on an opt-in basis, such as TypeScript[7] and C#. If your project uses one of these languages without being null safety-enabled, it can be challenging but worth it to migrate the code. Figma and VSCode are two examples of large projects in TypeScript that migrated their large codebase to enable null safety and permanently remove that source of bugs.[8]

- **Functional languages.** John Carmack, the creator of games such as Doom and Quake and a legend in the world of programming, has written that he believes functional programming is an approach that reduces the number of bugs by preventing issues related to state management. In his words, "It makes the state presented to your code explicit, which makes it much easier to reason about, and in a completely pure system makes thread race conditions impossible."[9]

    Functional programming languages are still fairly niche, which might unfortunately make them unsuitable for many organizations. However, more and more languages allow for the adoption of some functional programming techniques. John Carmack's article about the benefits of functional programming is actually based on examples of how he adopted some of these techniques in C++, a language that is not considered functional.

Choosing a Framework That Prevents Mistakes

The choice of software framework is as important as the choice of language. A framework is an abstraction above the language. It provides a standard way to build and deploy applications and gives the development teams many out-of-the-box functionalities that they can then further customize. Frameworks may include ready-made modules, code libraries, and toolsets and bring together all these components to facilitate the development of a project. Popular frameworks in web development include React, Django, Symfony, and Spring Boot. There are hundreds more.

As the name suggests, a framework frames the way you work, so you want it to contribute to preventing mistakes. Factors to take into account include:

- The maturity of the testing environment, to facilitate test-first programming.
- The soundness of its architecture, to make it easy to extend.
- The quality of the code inside the framework, if it's open source. Even if the development teams don't directly use that code, it serves as a model.
- The quality of the documentation, to allow development teams to easily use the framework as intended, rather than bend it in unintended ways that will have a negative effect on quality later on.

Having covered the shared foundations, let's look at what developers can do at the individual level.

Linters, Poka-Yokes for Code

Linters are the closest you can get to having a poka-yoke while coding. They are filters that analyze code while you are writing it or before you submit it to the rest of the team. These filters flag programming errors, bugs, stylistic errors, and suspicious constructs.[10] Linters are usually directly integrated in the development environment, just like an automatic spell-checker in a word processor (see Figures 12.1 and 12.2).

Linters include standard warnings created by the community. They can also include any custom rules the team comes up with. This makes them an amazing tool for teams to improve their development environment as a result of problem-solving past defects. If they can find a rule that would have prevented a defect, they can add it to the linter and share it with everyone on the team or in the organization.

Linters are meant to check the application of generic rules across the whole codebase. What about checking that individual functions are behaving as intended?

```
// total seconds since last modified
let deltaSeconds = useMemo(
  () => (updatedNowDate.getTime() - lastModifiedDate.getTime()) / MILLISECONDS_PER_SECOND,
  [lastModifiedDate, updatedNowDate],
);
```

FIGURE 12.1   Code without linter.

```
// total seconds since last modified
let deltaSeconds = useMemo(
  () => (updatedNowDate.getTime() - lastModifiedDate.getTime()) / MILLISECONDS_PER_SECOND,
  [lastModifiedDate, updatedNowDate],
);

(parameter) lastModifiedDate: Date | undefined
Object is possibly 'undefined'. ts(2532)
View Problem (⌥F8)    No quick fixes available
```

FIGURE 12.2   Code with a linter, detecting a null-unsafe operation.

Create a Test-Driven Development Environment

In 1999, Kent Beck and the Extreme programming movement popularized the concept of creating a test for each function written. Initially called "test-first programming," it eventually evolved into "test-driven development," or TDD.[11] For each increment of code, the idea is to first code the unit tests that will check whether the function you are about to create is doing what it is meant to do. Then code the actual function.

TDD encourages a discipline of auto-quality. Almost as a by-product, it generates a suite of auto-quality tests that can be run every time a change is introduced in the codebase, to detect unexpected side effects and prevent defects from being deployed into the product. In our experience, teams practicing TDD have a much lower defect rate.

Beyond the initial hurdle of getting familiar with TDD, the biggest obstacle to adoption typically lies within a development environment that doesn't make writing tests easy and quick. The most common challenges include:

1. Lack of test data, also known as "fixtures."
2. Lack of understanding and examples of how to "mock" certain services, especially when working within a framework. Mocking is a necessary aspect of testing that reduces the testing perimeter to the code being written, rather than extending it to the entire existing framework.

Investing in creating good fixtures for the project and adding examples or documentation on the specifics of testing within that project environment are key to making the adoption of test-driven development easier for the team.

Build on Top of the Organization's Best Practices

Digital is unique in allowing assets to be duplicated instantly and for free. A way to prevent mistakes is therefore to avoid writing new code in the first place by reusing existing code that has already been battle-tested.

A way to get that benefit is, again, to choose a good framework, so as to reuse code already tested and improved by a large community. That framework can also be enriched with shared libraries created internally by the teams, to integrate all the best practices learned over the years and reuse them as a foundation for every project.

At Theodo, we have Forge, a repository that contains our enriched versions of Django, NextJS, NestJS, and other frameworks we use. Forge is full of organization-specific best practices. It ensures that all teams, even the less experienced, start from a codebase that includes all the best practices our veterans have identified and implemented successfully in production before.

Industrial-Scale Quality

As software eats the world and enters more and more critical systems, we need to learn from Toyota how it transformed quality in the car manufacturing industry and can transform our tech industry the same way.

The scandal of the "firetrap" Ford Pinto in the 1970s captures the dismal state of quality in the car manufacturing industry at the time. Despite knowing that the Pinto's fuel tank might explode if a car crashed into it from behind, Ford decided to go ahead with the faulty design.

To make matters worse, Ford lobbied against stricter safety regulations, with a cost-benefit analysis arguing that safer designs would cost car manufacturers more than what the additional casualties would cost society. When the first car exploded, killing its occupants in a large fireball, the analysis was leaked to the press and the public was outraged. Regulators pressured Ford to recall 1.5 million cars.

That's the context in which the Toyota Corolla surged on the U.S. market. It was launched in 1968 and quickly recognized for its craftsmanship, finish, and overall build quality. It showed the American market that the highest quality could be affordable and redefined industry standards. As competitors scrambled to catch up, the number of U.S. fatalities per 100 million miles traveled dropped from 5.5 in 1966 to 3.5 in 1974 and 1.5 and less since 2000.

By showing the industry that the highest quality was achievable at industrial scale, Toyota raised standards and helped save millions of lives.

In the tech industry, we can take inspiration from Toyota. We can adopt a jidoka approach to detecting defects as early as possible (and stopping to fix them) and a dantotsu approach of learning from defects to exterminate them. This is how we will stop defects from reaching customers and users, increase our mastery to avoid defects, and redesign our working environments to prevent mistakes.

Of course we must be pragmatic and acknowledge the pressure to deliver. How can we make sure that quality doesn't come at the expense of cost and/or delivery speed? Or that quality efforts aren't sacrificed as soon as the deadline approaches? This is where we need to draw on the second pillar of the Toyota Production System: just-in-time.

PART FIVE

Deliver Continuously with Just-in-Time

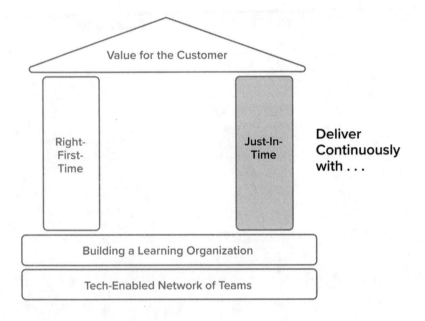

THE LOCKDOWN
SCALING STORY

At the beginning of 2020, when the Covid-19 pandemic lock-down started, one of the many unknowns was how businesses would deal with the impact of shutting down. In many countries, governments offered them immediate financial support. In France the BPI, the French public investment bank and one of our clients, was tasked with quickly creating the platform for providing state-guaranteed loans. We were given the opportunity to build it, on the condition of delivering within the next five days. Four and half days of hard work later, the platform was live[1] and $1 billion in loans went out over the following 24 hours.

After this initial success, the client asked our teams to expand on that work and build new products, including a multipurpose lending platform. As the workload and number of teams increased, the incredible velocity at which we had built the first platform soon became a distant memory. The teams were still delivering working software on a weekly schedule, but the deployment step was now taking more days than it had taken to build and deploy the whole initial platform. We were meeting deadlines, but only with heroic efforts that were draining the teams. Our client asked us to throw more and more developers at the problem. We weren't convinced this was the right approach, but we were too busy pushing harder to properly challenge that strategy.

When the stress became unbearable and our client finally expressed its dissatisfaction with the situation, we took a step back and assigned one of our best delivery experts to the problem. One of her first reactions was to introduce a kanban, to visualize all the work in progress and highlight the many steps where work was stuck "in waiting." This made the bottlenecks visible and helped build a plan to solve the issues.

This led us to invest in more modular architecture, clarify which team owned which module, create more automated tests to let teams deploy independently, and reduce work in progress.

Soon after, the weekly batched release was replaced by teams deploying on their own again, which further reduced work in progress. The organization went from 1 to 25 releases a week, and the change lead time dropped from up to 24 days to fewer than 10 days.

At scale, the Agile value of "working software over comprehensive documentation" is not enough guidance to coordinate the work of dozens of teams and maintain the very fast time-to-market of product innovation expected from Agile teams. Just-in-time, developed in manufacturing to improve production flow, brings with it decades of experience in addressing that problem.

Just-in-Time, the Most Counterintuitive Part of the Toyota Production System

Toyota first shared just-in-time (JIT) with the rest of the world in 1977. The company described it as the element of TPS that ensures "only the necessary products, at the necessary time, in necessary quantities are manufactured, and in addition, that the stock on hand is held down to a minimum."[2]

This is the part of TPS that features some of the most counterintuitive and therefore often misunderstood concepts. But this new way of looking at delivery flow has changed the world by helping most manufacturing organizations see problems that were invisible and to achieve shorter lead-time delivery in a more predictable way.

Some of Toyota's ideas have already reached the software industry, largely brought by the devops movement. However, it's worth going back to the original key principles to get a deeper understanding of how they work and how they support each other to reduce lead time in software.

Lead Time, the Key Measure Addressed by Just-in-Time

To fully understand the meaning of JIT and what value it brings to delivery, it is critical to first understand the concept of lead time.

Lead time is the elapsed time between a process's initiation and completion. For example, "commute lead time" would be the time between the moment you leave your house and the moment you arrive at your desk. Lead time includes any time spent waiting rather than traveling: waiting for the bus or the elevator, for instance.

In an organization, the most important lead time is customer lead time: the time that elapses between the placement of a customer order and the moment that customer finally gets to benefit from the product. This is not an interval that refers to a company's internal measurements—such as cycle time, for example, the time it takes to produce a product/service—but one that is based on the time as the customer experiences it. (See Figure 13.1.)

There are four main reasons why lead time is so important. Let's look at them.

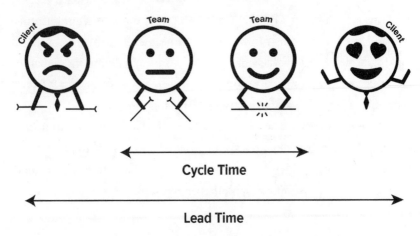

Cycle Time

Lead Time

FIGURE 13.1   Customer lead time versus cycle time.

Reason #1: A Shorter Lead Time Is a Huge, Often Untapped Source of Value for Customers

If you order a burger in a restaurant and it takes 30 minutes to arrive rather than 3 minutes, the perceived value of your eating-out experience will be much lower, even if it is exactly the same burger and served at the same temperature. That's because you wanted the burger 30 minutes ago, and what you got is a burger plus 30 minutes of waiting and frustration.

Reason #2: Aiming for a Shorter Lead Time Will Increase the Number of Learning Opportunities

A shorter lead time has the direct benefit of allowing for quicker, more frequent feedback loops. This is true with end customers, an idea that Agile and Lean startups have strongly defended as the key to learning faster from users and also internally. With shorter lead times comes an increased frequency in the number of feedback loops between different teams working together on the same product, which makes problems visible earlier in the work. Combined with a culture of right-first-time quality, these problems represent opportunities for teams to correct defects earlier and improve their overall collaboration.

In the restaurant example, striving to deliver burgers faster will force both the waiters and the cooks to look at previously ignored blockers.

For instance, maybe a poor kitchen layout causes delays and prevents the work from happening in a flow.

Reason #3: Aiming for Shorter Lead Time in a Context of High Customization Pulls the Organization Toward More Flexibility

If you are running a restaurant, the easier way to quickly deliver food to customers is to offer a very limited menu. This is the strategy some fast-food players use. They can manage enough inventory for each ingredient, and their workforce can learn to cook any meal in a very short period of time.

Conversely, if you want to offer your customers any meal they want, it will be harder to deliver fast. You will inevitably be missing some ingredients and cooking skills, which would significantly increase your lead time and very likely have a negative impact on quality as well.

There is a strong trade-off between high customization and lead time, and trying to achieve both will require an understanding of the delivery flow's flexibility issues. You will have to understand the process in depth and improve each step that can't currently react fast enough to sudden changes in demand.

The constraint of high customization is very strong in software, where every new feature can be unique. In this context, striving to shorten lead time surfaces interesting challenges, such as automating tasks that are often repeated, designing a flexible architecture, investing in reusable software modules, improving the knowledge management of your tech team, and so on. The result is a better-performing team delivering the features your customers want, faster and more efficiently.

Reason #4: A Shorter Lead Time Means Lower Costs

To deliver in a shorter lead time, an organization needs to find and reduce the waste in the value stream that prevented it from going faster. Reduced waste means reduced costs for the customer and the organizations.

Three Key Challenges to Reduce Lead Time

Now that we have established why lead time is so important, these are the three challenges that must be constantly addressed if you are to shorten your lead time:

- Help teams use a pull system to prioritize the value that the customer needs right now.
- Help teams limit work in progress with a one-piece flow.
- Help teams better synchronize their collaboration with takt time.

14

PULL: PRIORITIZE
THE VALUE THE
CUSTOMER NEEDS NOW

The Hidden Waste: Teams Working on Useless Tasks

A common problem encountered during go and sees is that teams are not prioritizing customer value. They are focused on doing a good job in their area of responsibility, while missing what is actually needed at the organizational level to deliver the most value to the customer.

For example, the product design team might be creating product specifications and wireframes for features that have not been prioritized yet. If things were to change, as they often do, this work might end up in the bin, which is both wasteful and disheartening for the teams who put in the time to do it.

Such wasted effort is usually the result of good intentions. It might happen when a team finds a way to be more productive. For example, a designer might create a design system that lets a team suddenly go through its backlog faster. As the team runs out of high-priority work, they start anticipating possible work to keep themselves busy, creating wireframes for potential future features, many of which will never be developed.

Unfortunately, this type of waste is very hard to spot for two reasons. First, the team producing the work feels good about moving forward faster than planned and doesn't see a problem. Second, the rest of the organization can't easily spot that work that, with everything digital, is hidden somewhere in the cloud. New files in a cloud folder or new tickets on a Trello board are invisible to most people in an organization.

The aim of a pull system is to achieve a situation in which the product design team can work on only what the organization actually needs. In the previous example, once the product design team has no more work required of it, it has no alternative but to stop working and consider that a problem. It may be counterintuitive that the best way to improve value flow is to ask some people to stop working, but at the organizational level, the priority is to make the problem visible and address the bottleneck, rather than working on potentially useless tasks.

Kanbans

In order for people to prioritize tasks that create value for the organization and its customers, it's critical to unequivocally clarify what work request is valuable right now.

When faced with a similar challenge at Toyota, Taiichi Ohno invented the *kanban*.[1] He imagined a solution where an upstream team would only work on a task in response to a request from the downstream team. To clarify that, he created a system based on a piece of cardboard that a team would give to another team to materialize a request. He called that system "kanban," which means "signboard" in Japanese.

As an example, consider a team on the assembly line that needs a new box of 10 side mirrors for a certain car model. It orders the box from the team that produces the side mirrors by giving that team a kanban cardboard with all the relevant details. The side-mirror production team stores the kanban in a "kanban launcher" and works on the kanban requests in the exact order received.

When the 10 side mirrors are finished and put in a box, the production team takes the kanban cardboard that was in the launcher, puts it on the box, and sends the box back to the ordering team. When the box is empty again, the first team reuses the kanban cardboard to order the next box of side mirrors. This ensures the work requested to the upstream team is continuously connected to the actual needs of the downstream team.

These kanban cardboards, connecting every team in the value stream, cascade the priorities to everyone in the organization.

The flow of kanban connects the whole value stream from the customer all the way to the materials. The kanban acts as a communication tool between all those teams, creating a direct connection between the needs of the customers and the work plan of every team in the flow. Ideally, all your teams should be connected this way, starting from the initial customer request.

The Pull System

The concept of kanban has been popular in software since 2010, with David Anderson's book *Kanban: Successful Evolutionary Change for Your Technology Business.*[2] Inspired by Toyota's original kanban, Anderson focused on making work in progress visible on a board and enforcing flow constraints in the flow to take into account each team's work capacity. We can implement this with a popular project management tool such as Jira or Trello. The "card" or "ticket" acts as the kanban signboard, and different workflow columns represent the different teams that need to work on that feature.

Yet most of the kanbans we have seen in digital fail to enable a proper pull system. They are typically missing three features that are key to identifying problems in the flow and empowering teams to solve them: inventory, where pieces of work are waiting instead of being worked on; the lead time of each piece of work; and which people or teams are working on which piece of work. By making those three visible, the team can immediately identify excess inventory, which pieces have excessive lead time, and which person or team is the current bottleneck. By solving these three types of issues as they appear, teams can maintain a good workflow.

In short, to make a digital kanban a "real" kanban, it needs three features: (1) inventory columns where cards go when they are waiting to move from one step to another, (2) digital kanban cards that display the lead time since the card's creation, and (3) columns that correspond to teams in the flow rather than steps in a process. (See Figure 14.1.)

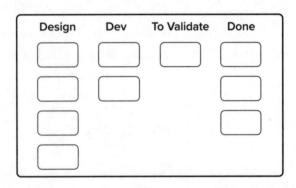

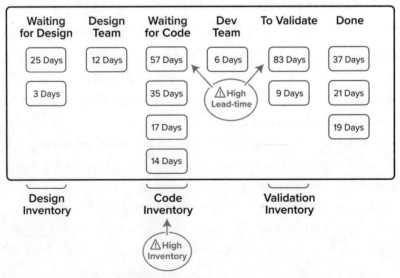

FIGURE 14.1   Kanban with inventory columns and lead times.

Local Versus Global Optimization

The pull system helps the teams work on the global priority rather than what they locally believe to be a priority. This is a typical problem of local versus global optimization, which one can illustrate with a range of mountains: the team is doing its best to get to the top of the hill it knows and is in charge of, unaware that the organization should collectively go to a different mountain to reach the highest peak. (See Figure 14.2.)

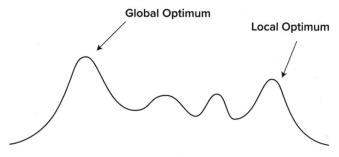

FIGURE 14.2   Local and global optimization.

A kanban helps teams focus on the global priorities, breaking silos by connecting demand between teams and identifying problems in the organizational flow. But how do we ensure that flow problems don't reappear within the teams?

ONE-PIECE FLOW: HELP TEAMS LIMIT WORK IN PROGRESS

There are many ways for a team to operate that are not best for the overall organization. In a factory, the classic example is *batching*, a method that produces a large set of items in a row, repeating each step multiple times. Batching is very common. It's tempting for a production cell to run its machine at full speed for days to produce thousands of copies of the same part, locally maximizing production before producing thousands of copies of the next part. Batching feels right locally, because it allows the team to blaze through a single step repeatedly. Unfortunately, it has side effects at the organization level:

- Batching creates larger problems. If there is a production issue, you have to discard all the parts in the batch.
- Batching creates rigidity in production. If the customer or another team needs a different part quickly, they will have to wait until the end of the batch.

- Few batches are needed all at once. In the meantime, they will have to be stored somewhere, requiring additional space.
- The larger the batch, the more money invested to produce it and the longer it will take to sell it. While the goods are not sold, they are inventory. A business runs better when investments are turned into cash quickly, rather than into more inventory.

Local Optimization in Software Engineering

In software engineering, there is an equivalent to batching: a team working on multiple features at the same time. Locally, this feels better to the team members: it allows each member to work on a different feature, avoiding treading on anyone else's toes.

In reality, a step back lets you see the negative effects of this approach. For instance, take a team working in sprints using the Scrum methodology. In Scrum, a sprint is a short, time-boxed period, typically one to four weeks, when a Scrum team works to complete a set amount of work. To better separate the workload and work more efficiently, a team of three developers might decide to take on three features instead of one in the sprint.

They each split their feature into smaller increments and complete perhaps 80 percent of each feature by the end of the sprint. They might feel that they have produced more efficiently by working uninterrupted on their individual features. But none of the features are finished, they are not deployed, and the customer has received no value. They have delayed the delivery of value to the customer by at least another sprint—an additional one to four weeks.

One-Piece Flow in Digital

In Lean, the solution to this problem is called "one-piece flow." It is a way to ensure teams adopt the delivery discipline of focusing on what is best for the customer first and avoid local optimizations that feel good to the team but are detrimental to the customer. In our example, establishing one-piece flow means moving from working on multiple features in parallel and delivering bits of each feature at the end of each sprint to working on one feature at a time. (See Figure 15.1.)

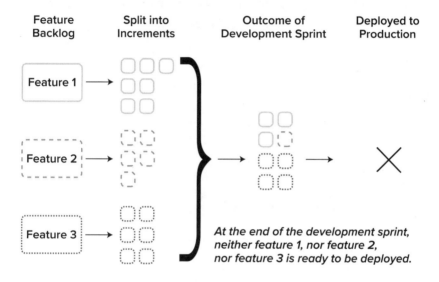

With One-Piece Flow

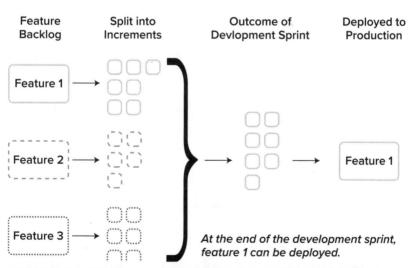

FIGURE 15.1 Working on multiple features in parallel and deploying none, compared to focusing on one feature at a time with one-piece flow.

With this system, each feature is delivered as early as possible. The riskiest tasks within a feature are not postponed, and the team works together on the same feature, thus creating more shared ownership and allowing for more frequent mutual quality checks.

This does require going against the natural inclination to avoid treading on each other's toes, which may be especially strong in software engineering, an industry that usually attracts introverts.

The change can be made progressively, by first introducing one-task flow at the developer level, then ensuring this is supported by a one-branch flow at the code level (better known as "trunk-based development"), and finally aiming for one-feature flow at the team level.

One-Task Flow for Every Developer

We started with one-task flow at Theodo. In our early days of Agile, we adopted the 2010 Scrum guide's recommendation that we decompose items to less than one day of work.[1] We also introduced the rule of maximum one item per developer in the "doing column." This proved very effective against batching and tunneling.

"Batching" in a software context is when a developer works on multiple tasks in parallel to quickly complete very similar subtasks. For example, a developer might work on all the subtasks in the backlog that require a change to the same class. This reduces context switching, but at a cost: now there are multiple unfinished tasks in progress.

Tunneling is another concept frequently seen in software engineering. Developers who tunnel work for days (or even weeks!) on a task without telling the rest of the team where they are and how it's going.

Batching and tunneling are against the Scrum pillars of transparency and inspection. Tasks that stay "in progress" for a long time prevent problems from surfacing and team members from helping.

Conversely, moving to a one-task flow for each developer, combined with the discipline of breaking down tasks in increments of less than a day, will empower the team members to submit their work every day to the rest of the team and give full visibility on their progress and any issues they might encounter.

Of course, introducing one-task flow will reveal some problems, like:

- "Both tasks require similar code. I want to work on both at the same time."
- "I am waiting for the code review from someone else on the first increment, so I would rather start something new than stay idle."
- "The first task can't be finished without this second one."

These are all great opportunities for problem solving, which will help improve the flow: for example, creating a dependency graph to help developers better plan the sequence of work or improving teamwork on code reviews.

Trunk-Based Development

A one-task-flow approach is not enough if it is not supported by a one-branch-flow approach at the code level. Ever since Git became the leading code versioning system to help developers collaborate on the same codebase, maintaining multiple branches of the same codebase has become much easier and therefore much more common. Code branches are alternative versions of the codebase that allow developers to start new work on a codebase while not affecting its original version, usually named the "trunk" or "main branch." Creating new, temporary branches, working on them, and later merging them back into the main branch has become an essential part of development flow.

The downside is that it is now common for someone's work in progress to live within a branch that the rest of the team doesn't look at or can't even access. If multiple branches evolve independently for too long, it will become difficult to merge them back into the main branch, as separate contributions to similar places in the code will contradict each other and result in merge conflicts. More important, excessive branching is a barrier to collaboration. It lets developers keep code to themselves for days or weeks on end. Quite ironic, given that Git is meant to help developers collaborate on a shared codebase.

The one-piece-flow principle is also relevant here and can address these negative side effects by ensuring that all the work in progress flows through a single branch. Tech thought leaders who support trunk-based development, including Paul Hammant,[2] Martin Fowler,[3] Jez Humble, and Dave Farley,[4] have advocated for exactly this. With trunk-based development, team members commit to trunk at least once every 24 hours.

Just as they challenge one-task flow, coders often challenge trunk-based development, saying "My code is not ready to be merged," or "I am waiting for someone to review the pull-request before merging." Again, these are all interesting problems to solve in order to improve flow and collaboration. It's a place to introduce good practices, such as feature toggling to merge unfinished features. Its adoption at a very large scale by Google and Facebook is proof that trunk-based development is not just for small teams.

One-Feature Flow for Every Team

Once a team understands the benefits of the one-piece-flow principle, it's time to adopt one-piece flow at the feature level, so both the organization and customer can get the full benefit. This means limiting the number of features in progress to a maximum of one (or two) within each team. This requires a lot of teamwork, as people need to come out of their bubbles and work more closely with fellow team members.

The problems typically encountered here include:

- "We started working on a new feature because we are waiting for the UX team to come back on the first one."

One-Piece Flow: Help Teams Limit Work in Progress   131

- "The feature can't be deployed until another feature is done."
- "Working on these multiple features in parallel saves us time."

Problem-solving these impediments will foster collaboration between different teams and uncover a lot of wasted time that was previously invisible. Some examples:

- Realizing that the development team never uses half of the wireframes produced by the UX team.
- Realizing that the team consistently loses one week of lead time because translators lack tooling to work directly within the developer's environment.
- Creating a consistent design system in both Figma (for designers) and React (for developers) so that both teams can work much more efficiently together.

The Necessity of a Flexible Working Environment

The cost of context switching is one of the typical counterarguments to implementing one-piece flow:

- "Why not work on all front-end-related subtasks at once, now that I have made the effort to download the front-end code and set up my working environment for it?"
- "Why not finish all the tasks and deploy them together, since every deployment takes ages?"
- "Why not combine all the migrations to the database structure together, since we depend on the database administrator to implement them?"

These are symptoms of an inflexible working environment. Ideally, setting up the front-end development environment, deploying to production, or migrating the database should take only minutes. This would be much more conducive to one-piece flow and would also make it easier to onboard someone exterior to the team.

Flexible Machines in a Factory: SMED

Factories often have visible examples of a similar lack of flexibility. A big press that molds a certain part will need to be reconfigured to mold a different part. Changing the part's die and reconfiguring the machine to fit the new die will take hours or days. On such equipment, the intuitive choice is to produce parts in batches that run longer than the time required to change the press, to offset the initial time invested in changing the die and reconfiguring the machine.

That lack of flexibility has direct consequences, however. If the team downstream asks for different parts to be delivered every hour, and the upstream team takes hours just to change the die, the requirement can only be satisfied by having a large inventory of the different parts acting as a buffer.

Toyota saw a huge opportunity here early on. If it could work with the operators on reducing changeover times, it would reduce inventory and save cash with little downside. Toyota accumulated years of experience in completing tasks that seemed to require hours of work in mere minutes, thanks to techniques that later came to be known as single-minute exchange of die (SMED).[5]

Nowadays it is even possible to get rid of the die-changing step with 3-D printing, also called "additive manufacturing." SpaceX made extensive use of it to have total flexibility on the design of its engine parts and iterate much faster on its Merlin and Super Draco engines.[6]

SMED in Tech

In tech, a lack of flexibility in our machines is less visible but not less important. The devops movement highlighted how making deployment quicker increased deployment frequency and avoided the temptation of batching feature delivery.

Amazon is a great example of this.[7] In 2009, its deployment process was already well instrumented, but not automated. Deployment from code check-in to production was taking an average of 16 days.

Considering that the typical increment was built in one or two days, this meant that waiting for deployment was taking 90 percent of the total time. Not only was this incredibly wasteful, but Amazon had by now also learned that it had an effect on retaining senior software engineers, who were fed up with the impediments. It decided to react and create an environment where "builders can build."

Looking at these 16 days, it was easy to see that the organization spent less than an hour on actually compiling and deploying new code, and spent almost 14 days waiting for team members to start a build, perform deployments, or run tests. A new platform called "Pipelines" automated all these steps. It had to automate the process in a way that increased confidence versus the old method, and included more automated testing, staggered production deployment, and allowed easy rollback in case of problems.

Once this was all automated, it reduced total deployment time by 90 percent. As an interesting side effect, the teams that adopted Pipelines also started releasing one change at a time. Just as with SMED at Toyota, shortening the time to deployment at Amazon made it easier for teams to adopt a single-piece deployment flow and deliver value much earlier and much more frequently.

Less Work in Progress Helps the Flow

The pull system and single-piece flow focus the organization on the flow of value. This helps teams and individuals understand the organization's and customer's priorities and contribute much more directly to it. Rather than working on local priority, leading to a lot of unnecessary work in progress, the organization works together on what is needed now, which improves the flow.

But it doesn't guarantee that the organization is well sized for the flow. If a team is too small and becomes the bottleneck of the rest of the organization, the pull system would make this problem visible. But how can we find a way to anticipate these bottlenecks and size teams accordingly?

人16

TAKT TIME: SYNCHRONIZE TEAM COLLABORATION

Take Time to Define the Ideal Flow

Having one or more underresourced teams in the flow is the equivalent of a pipe becoming much narrower at some point, resulting in constant clogging. To address this in the plumbing world would require making sure the pipe has the same diameter throughout. In the real world, the solution is actually similar: resize the different teams so that on average, they deliver their increments at the same pace.

Consider two teams that are part of a flow delivering features. For example, imagine a front-end team coding a feature's user interface and a back-end team coding the API part of that feature. If the front-end team delivers its contribution in an average of seven days and the back-end team is done in an average of three days, then the back-end team will have to wait four days to be useful again. On average, that will happen every seven days.

The most straightforward solution to that problem, if the teams are small enough, is to merge the two teams into a full-stack team. This makes it easier for the team to self-organize. If the back end is built faster than the front end, assuming that back-end and front-end devs can help each other, they will be able to give each other a hand instead of waiting. This is one of the reasons the ideal product team is a cross-functional team with front-end, back-end, product, design, and infrastructure skills working closely together and helping each other.

If the teams are too large to consider merging them, then we need to organize them along a flow. And to make sure that teams along the same flow are sized correctly, you can determine the target pace and size each team to match that target. For example, in an organization working in one-week sprints, the target pace could be one feature per sprint. Every week a feature will pass from one team to another, and a fully finished feature will come out of the delivery flow, like clockwork. This is why Toyota call this interval "takt time"—from the German word *Takt*, which means "beat time."

Delivery organizations rarely run like clockwork. Introducing a takt time and reorganizing teams to deliver at that pace will not solve all clogging problems by itself. However, it will improve the average situation and highlight problems whenever the situation is not average. Typical issues it can reveal include:

- Too much variability in feature size, which product management can address by splitting features in similar-sized increments
- A team's lack of competence on a certain topic, slowing it down, which we can address through targeted training or by asking an expert to help
- A need for temporary reinforcement, which we can address on the tech side with pair programming or mob programming around a particularly difficult task

Takt Time to Problem-Solve More Frequently

Takt time is great to synchronize the different teams working in a flow. It is also useful in aiming for a more stable work rhythm at different levels. For example, when Facebook pushes new code to production every few hours,[1] it ensures that deploying to production becomes a regular activity happening throughout the day with a stable takt time. If at some point that doesn't happen, it's a visible problem that can be solved.

Similarly, the burndown chart recommended in the early days of Scrum is a good example of having daily takt time at the team level (see Figure 16.1). By having teams update their progress on a graph every day and check whether they are delivering faster or more slowly than their target, it fosters the healthy practice of splitting work into increments that can be coded in less than a day. Any deviation from that takt time becomes a visible problem that the team can react to and solve.

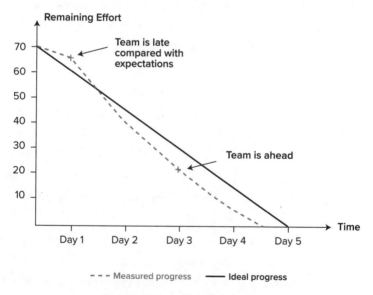

FIGURE 16.1   Burndown chart.

On a larger time scale, a good example is Apple's releases of a new version of its iPhone every year. By having a takt time of one year for new versions, it makes innovation a regular activity in the organization, rather than the unpredictable breakthrough it sometimes is.

In all these examples, takt time can be a powerful tool to level workload. It helps plan for the expected pace and makes excessive variations from that pace visible problems that can be analyzed and solved.

Debunking the Misconception That Just-in-Time Is About Reducing Inventory

Before we conclude this chapter on just-in-time, we must address a common misconception. Just-in-time is still too often considered a method to reduce costs by aggressively lowering inventory.[2] The Covid-19 crisis brought this criticism back, with several articles published in newspapers[3] and magazines that blamed just-in-time for the lack of personal protective equipment at the beginning of the pandemic and an inability to cope with a sudden spike in demand, resulting in very long lead times.

The term "just-in-time" can give the impression that this strategy is about doing things at the last minute, only once a need is identified. It is rather about learning how to improve delivery with better collaboration within the flow and finding more opportunities to make delivery issues visible. What the Covid-19 crisis actually highlighted is the supply chain's lack of flexibility and a dearth of scenario planning around a potential health emergency, despite multiple warnings in the previous 25 years.[4] This was a symptom of focusing on cost reduction rather than on the learning and resilience of just-in-time.

For Toyota, the inventor of just-in-time, the Covid-19 crisis was an opportunity to demonstrate what good just-in-time and the resulting deep understanding of its supply chain and investment in resilience look like. In 2021, a postpandemic computer chip shortage hit the car industry. A March 2021 *Guardian* article[5] reported the resulting plant shutdowns were projected to cost Ford up to $2.5 billion and General Motors up to $2 billion.

Not Toyota, which surprised rivals and investors when it told the markets its output would not be disrupted significantly.[6] When the chip shortage hit, Toyota had already addressed that key risk in its supply chain, allowing it to be one of the only carmakers thriving during the crisis. The group achieved a record year in revenue, operating profit, and net income,[7] capturing more market shares from its closest competitor, Volkswagen.[8]

Continuous Delivery to Shorten the Learning Cycle

Agile tells us that we should "deliver working software frequently." Indeed, the challenges of software delivery are best addressed through trial and error, striving to deliver and solving issues along the way, rather than by investing time in long specifications.

But with scale, "working software" doesn't address the slowdown due to bad coordination between an increased number of teams contributing to the software.

With a track record of delivering superior quality in record time and at industrial scale, the Toyota Production System and its two pillars of right-first-time and just-in-time give us a more comprehensive approach to scale delivery excellence.

They also demonstrate that the constraint triangle between quality, speed, and cost can be broken. An organization that successfully strives to radically improve both quality and speed will end up with reduced costs. Toyota did in the 1970s, and tech giants such as Amazon, Google, and Meta did in the 2000s, when they surprised competitors by delivering a service that was better, faster, and cheaper.

Delivering better, faster, and cheaper is not the only reason tech companies have disrupted traditional organizations. What made them successful in the first place is the radical innovations they were bringing to their markets.

Delivering more often allowed them to iterate more frequently on their products, creating more opportunities to learn how customer needs were changing and innovate faster than traditional organizations. *The Lean Startup* captured this idea very well by promoting the idea of releasing a minimum viable product early and iterating quickly on the build ⟶ measure ⟶ learn cycle.

The challenge when the organization becomes larger is to scale that innovation capability. Iterating on a product will improve it incrementally, but will not be sufficient for a large organization to step back, understand what its customers really need, and identify the new and large-enough markets it must address to gain market share. Even when it does, the organization still needs to learn to succeed in those new markets. To continue innovating at scale, an organization cannot just rely on quick iteration—it needs to build a learning organization.

PART SIX

Continue Innovating by Building a Learning Organization

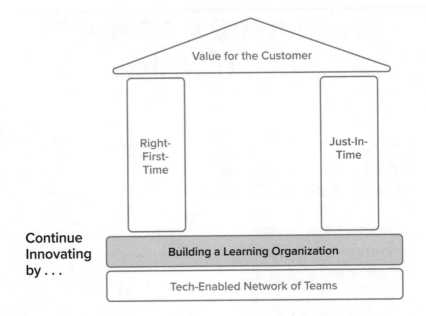

17

AMAZON VERSUS GOOGLE ON INNOVATION

Amazon and Google, Champions of Responding to Change

I f we had to pick the companies that best embody the ability to respond to change at scale, rather than following a plan, Amazon and Google would probably top the list.

Of course, to respond to change, you must first be able to detect it. In that domain, both organizations excel. They are extremely attentive to their users' needs and have scaled that capability by systematically collecting and analyzing data about user behavior.

In 2009 Marissa Mayer, who was in charge of Google.com's home page at the time, made A/B testing popular when she told the American Institute of Graphic Arts design conference how Google used this process to understand what users preferred and automate many of its design decisions.[1] A/B testing consists of showing a version A of the product to a set of users and a version B to another set of users, then measuring which one performs best. Mayer's team used A/B testing extensively to understand user preferences, replacing intuition with data-driven decisions. Her team even leveraged A/B testing to pick the optimal shade of blue for Google's ad links out of 41 different shades, reportedly generating an additional $200 million in annual ad revenue.[2]

Amazon also collects extensive statistical data from user behavior, driven by a desire to detect as many new business opportunities as possible. This can be traced back all the way to Jeff Bezos's own obsession with avoiding missed opportunities, which Bezos called "errors of omission." To prevent these, Amazon invested a lot of energy in its ability to make more bets, by lowering the cost of experimenting with new ideas. This is the role of Weblab, a platform that can run thousands of experiments on the website cheaply, collect data on the changes that work best for users,[3] and decide whether or not an opportunity is worth pursuing.

Both Google and Amazon have also developed incredible capabilities to respond quickly to changes in user behavior.

At the 2011 Velocity conference, Amazon's engineering teams said they were pushing changes to production every 11.6 seconds, or around 300 hundred times an hour. On average, these changes affected tens of thousands of servers at each deployment.[4]

Similarly, Google has created a state-of-the-art infrastructure to support high-velocity software engineering and deployment to production. Its centralized code source repository, with two billion lines of code on which all Google engineers can collaborate, seamlessly deals with changes to tens of millions of lines of code every week. That's 25 lines of code changed every second.[5] And like Amazon, Google invested in its continuous deployment pipeline. For example, the "push-on-green" system introduced in one service in 2014 accelerated the deployment of changes to production from a previous average of 10 to 20 times a month to 160 times a month.[6]

The ability to learn better from users' changing behaviors and respond faster than competitors has helped Google and Amazon grow tremendously over the past 25 years. Nonexistent in 1995, these two companies have created more than $1 trillion in market capitalization. They are now two of the five biggest companies and two of the top three most valuable brands in the world.[7]

Amazon Beats Google in Building Sustainable Innovation

When you look more closely at outcomes in terms of innovation, there's however a major difference between the success rate of the two companies' newly released products. For example, Google has tried to innovate in the direct messaging space and released or acquired 10 different products over the last 15 years. Only one of them survives: Google Messages/RCS, created in 2019. The rest have been terminated: Google Talk (2005–2013), Meebo (2005–2012), Google Wave (2009–2012), Google Buzz (2010–2011), Google+ (2011–2019), Google Hangouts (2013–2022), Google Spaces (2016–2017), Google Allo (2016–2019), and YouTube Messages (2017–2019). That's a 10 percent success rate.

This track record goes beyond messaging products. At the time of writing, Google has killed 293 products, including better-known products such as Stadia, Inbox, Picasa, Orkut, Google Reader, Google Wave, and Google Desktop. Since Google launched, it has killed one product each month on average, inspiring the creation of the meme website https://killedbygoogle.com.

On the other hand, Amazon has successfully launched hundreds of products that had nothing to do with its initial core business of online retail.

The story of the Kindle is one such example. Seeing the rising demand for digital content, Amazon decided to respond with a dedicated team. And instead of looking at its existing capabilities and assets to decide what to do, Amazon started from the customer.

Focusing on the digital reading experience, the team agreed that a great customer experience required inventing a new reading device. Untroubled by the fact that it was an e-commerce company with no prior experience in making hardware, Amazon invested in learning how to build a device and created the Kindle. Fifteen years later, the Kindle has 75 percent of the market, and Amazon sells more than 100 million e-books every year.

The Kindle's success was not a stroke of luck. Amazon has demonstrated this ability to succeed in totally new markets many more times. For example, the AWS cloud continues to impress, 15 years after its launch. It started as an online retailer deciding to create an enterprise infrastructure business. Not only did it invent the cloud in the process, but it generated $62 billion revenue and $19 billion profit in 2021, or 13 percent of Amazon's total revenue and 75 percent of its total operating income.[8]

In comparison, Google's operating income in the fourth quarter of 2022 was still entirely generated by its advertisement business, its primary source of revenue since 2000.[9] The cloud and other bets were still losing money, dinging operating income by 15 percent.

The markets recognize this difference. Between 2015 and 2022, Amazon's price-to-earnings ratio, which measures a company's current valuation relative to its earnings, has been five times higher on average and never less than two times higher for Amazon than it is for Google. Investors expect more future growth from Amazon than from Google.

The Difference: Amazon Is a Learning Organization

Google and Amazon are great at responding to change over following a plan, a key success factor in the fast-paced tech industry. But there is something in Amazon's culture that makes it more successful at sustainable innovation than Google and most other companies.

As any innovative company probably should, Amazon has had its fair share of spectacular failures, such as the Amazon Fire phone.[10] Jeff Bezos captured it well in his 2018 letter to shareholders:

As a company grows, *everything* needs to scale, including the size of your failed experiments. If the size of your failures isn't growing, you're not going to be inventing at a size that can actually move the needle. Amazon will be experimenting at the right scale for a company of our size if we occasionally have multibillion-dollar failures.[11]

In that letter, Bezos also revealed some of Amazon's learning culture: "While the Fire phone was a failure, we were able to take our learnings (as well as the developers) and accelerate our efforts building Echo and Alexa."

But more often than its competitors, Amazon succeeds at entering new markets. It does so by learning what the customers need and acquiring as an organization the right skills to transform itself accordingly. This makes it a learning organization.[12]

The Challenges of Building a Learning Organization

We often describe Lean thinking as a learning system plugged into our existing production system, capable of turning every single production problem into a learning opportunity.

And indeed Lean thinking provides a framework to build a customer-led learning organization. It helps us:

- Learn what customers need, through a culture of problem solving, continuous experimentation, and deep customer empathy
- Build on past learnings by keeping teams stable, encouraging written standards, and learning from others
- Keep updating those learnings with kaizen
- Spread the learnings throughout the organization with Obeyas, a self-service data architecture, effective training programs, and communities of practice

人18

LEARN WHAT CUSTOMERS NEED

The famous quote attributed to Henry Ford—"If I had asked people what they wanted, they would have said faster horses"—is a powerful reminder that learning what customers need is not just about asking them. It is about understanding their problems and how to address them better than they can themselves.

The best place to start is by learning from the frustrations customers already have. By embedding problem solving into an organization's culture, we make it a reflex for everyone to listen to customer frustrations, then analyze and ideally fix them.

The next step is to experiment with what could actually improve the customer experience. Experimentation and problem solving are similar in their approach, but where problem solving aims to bring the situation back to normal, experimentation looks at which variations on the normal situation improve the customer experience.

Finally, to learn what customers need but don't yet know they need, we must think beyond the organization's existing capabilities and assets. We must use techniques to develop deep empathy for customers, to understand why they want a faster horse.

Problem-Solving Culture

We have already defined problem solving and how team leaders can better support and empower their teams by coaching them on it. But what makes problem solving become a systematic part of a culture?

To make it systematic, a leadership team must make surfacing problems a natural part of the work culture. To quote Taiichi Ohno, it must convince everyone that "having no problems is the biggest problem of all."

Bill Gates's Most Important Job Is to Listen for Bad News

Microsoft's Bill Gates is a great example of this. In his book *Business @ the Speed of Thought*, he wrote, "I think my most important job as CEO is to listen for bad news. If you don't act on it, your people will eventually stop bringing bad news to your attention. And that's the beginning of the end."

As Gates further explains, for this culture to materialize, the leadership team has to lead by example:

> A change in corporate attitude, encouraging and listening to bad news, has to come from the top. The CEO and the other senior executives have to insist on getting bad news, and they have to create an appetite for bad news throughout their organizations. The bearer of bad tidings should be rewarded, not punished. Business leaders have to want to listen to alerts from salespeople, product developers, and customers. You can't just turn off the alarm and go back to sleep. Not if you want your company to survive.

This means the leadership team needs to demonstrate to everyone in the organization a commitment to:

- Welcoming problems by thanking the person who flagged the problem and listening to that person with curiosity, without casting blame or suggesting guilt

- Analyzing problems by taking the time to coach employees on better understanding the identified issues

It's fine not to analyze every single problem. Still, this needs to be the exception (even for small problems), to avoid demotivating people from raising issues in the future.

Keeping Cool with Problems

When the problem is particularly bad and caused by a combination of mindless mistakes, it is hard to welcome it rather than pin the blame on those who made the mistakes. But it is exactly in those circumstances that leaders have an opportunity to define their organizational culture by demonstrating that even in the face of big mistakes, the intensity will be on what we can learn from the problem.

To stay positive when somebody brings up yet another problem, remember that the problem existed before you heard about it. First, it shows someone in your organization cares and is courageous enough to surface problems. And if the problem was not bad enough to stop the organization from functioning until now, now at least you can react and solving it will only make things better.

Embedding Problem Solving into the Culture

Welcoming problems and addressing them are staples of the cultures at both Toyota and Amazon.

In his book *Welcome Problems, Find Success*, Kiyoshi "Nate" Furuta, former chair and CEO of Toyota Boshoku America Inc., describes Toyota leaders and managers as asking "What is your problem?" thousands of times a year.

At Amazon, too, making sure problems are not ignored is a key leadership principle. This states that "Leaders ensure that defects do not get sent down the line and that problems are fixed so they stay fixed."[1]

At Theodo, different elements help embed welcoming and analyzing problems into our culture. Examples include:

- At our all-hands meeting on Monday mornings, called Asakai, we openly talk about customer problems to remind everyone that problems are OK.
- Leaders are expected to thank anyone surfacing a problem and offer help to coach the person on problem solving.
- When more senior leaders make mistakes, they are not blamed for them, but are expected to quickly share their problem solving.
- Projects have a problem-solving sheet, which can be an A3 piece of paper or a Notion table, listing the team's latest problem-solving exercises. This creates transparency and accountability around problem solving.
- Leadership teams' go and see visits to the front line are also an opportunity for leaders to show sincere interest in the problems the teams face and to dive into their problem-solving efforts.

Our problem-solving efforts help us better understand our customers. What's more, they actually love seeing our teams react to their problems, analyze them, and come up with ways to address them. But we can't just rely on problem solving to learn what customers need.

Product Development as a Continuous Experiment

While problem solving helps identify priorities by focusing on frustrating abnormalities, we also need to think creatively about the customer's experience. Tech products give us the amazing opportunity to continue evolving our product long after it has been bought. Every change deployed to production lets us experiment directly with the customer's experience and turn product development into a continuous experiment.

Good Ideas Have a Very Low Success Rate

The best product organizations in tech are those that have understood that every product change is an experiment with a high chance of failure. Ronny Kohavi, who directed Amazon's Data Mining and Personalization group before joining Microsoft as general manager of its Experimentation Platform, reveals a humbling statistic: in organizations that actually measure whether new ideas improve the metrics they were intended to improve, the success rate is below 50 percent.

Based on his own experiments at Microsoft,[2] Kohavi says that one-third of ideas create a statistically significant positive change, one-third produce no statistically significant difference, and one-third create a statistically significant negative change. And these are obviously not randomly selected ideas, but what experienced teams had deemed good enough to build and deploy. Similarly, Booking.com runs more than 1,000 rigorous tests simultaneously and an estimated 25,000 tests a year. Its measured success rate is 10 percent.[3]

These numbers are from product organizations that are mature enough to measure their ideas' success rates. For those that don't measure that rate and are therefore unable to learn by comparing their assumptions with reality, the success rate is probably lower. To avoid wasting a lot of effort on the wrong ideas, it is vital to turn product development into continuous experimentation. This means seeing every change as an experiment and an opportunity for the product team to learn whether its product hypothesis was right.

To implement continuous experimentation in product development, it is useful to distinguish between two phases: product discovery and product delivery.

Experimentation During Product Discovery

Product discovery is the phase during which we can run very quick and inexpensive experiments, using prototypes rather than the actual product. Such experiments can be carried out entirely offline.

Take the example of Jenn Hyman and Jenny Fleiss, the founders of Rent the Runway. After having the idea of renting designer clothes online for special occasions, they didn't rush to raise money and build the website. They first wanted to validate some of their major hypotheses. Would affluent young women rent designer dresses available at one-tenth of the retail price? Would they return them in good condition? To answer these questions, Hyman and Fleiss found 130 designer dresses and set up an experiment to rent them to Harvard undergrads. Of the 140 women who came in to view the dresses, 35 percent ended up renting one, and 51 out of the 53 renters mailed them back in good condition. The other two dresses had stains that were easily removed.

The results of the experiment were reassuring and led to the next question: Would women rent dresses they can't try on? To answer that, Hyman and Fleiss set up another experiment, this time on the Yale campus, letting women see the dresses before renting them, but not letting them try on the clothes. The second trial also had more dress options, because the first pilot revealed that many women did not rent because they couldn't find options they liked. The Yale pilot showed two things: women would rent dresses when they couldn't try them on, and the percentage of women who rented increased to more than 55 percent when they had more options.

Hyman and Fleiss had not yet written a single line of code, but they had already learned a lot about their market and validated some major hypotheses. Before building the website, they decided to test one last big question: Would women rent dresses they could not physically see? They took photos of each dress and ran a test in New York, where 1,000 women in the target audience got the option to rent a dress after seeing a photo of it. This final experiment showed that roughly 5 percent of women looking for special-occasion dresses were willing to try the service, enough to reassure Hyman and Fleiss about the viability of renting high fashion over the web.[4] They validated their first major hypothesis without any tech investment at all.

Rent the Runway is now a leading fashion tech startup. It went public on the Nasdaq in 2021 and generated $280 million in annual revenue in 2022.

There are many ways to carry out quick experiments during product discovery, whether it's fully offline like Rent the Runway, or using online prototyping tools such as spreadsheets or a patchwork of no-code SaaS solutions. During product discovery, testing hypotheses can and should be very cheap. Leverage simple prototypes and show them to a small group of beta testers, such as colleagues or carefully selected customers.

In *Inspired*, Marty Cagan gives an idea of how quick such experiments need to be. "Strong teams normally test many product ideas each week—in the order of 10 to 20 or more per week." This number can seem daunting, especially when you start from zero. It makes more sense once you understand that we are talking about breaking down big ideas into many small hypotheses and then into further tests focused on the four critical product risks:

1. **Value.** Will the user buy this idea or choose to use it?
2. **Usability.** Can we make this idea practical for the user?
3. **Feasibility.** Can our engineers build this idea?
4. **Business viability.** Can our stakeholders support this idea?

This breakdown helps the product discovery team run many small tests every week to generate multiple "validated learnings," learnings based on evidence. This is how the team refines its deep understanding and intuition of what works and what doesn't.

Experimentation During Product Delivery

Once quick experiments run during discovery have provided evidence that something is worth building, delivery comes in. In the right working environment, the product delivery team should be able to ship a feature to production in one to two weeks. The team should also be empowered on using analytics or an A/B testing platform to determine whether the feature, once in production, improves the metric it was meant to improve.

At Booking.com, for example, a centralized experimentation infra- structure enables every employee to experiment on millions of customers without getting permission from management. This includes anything from adding a new feature on a page of the website to testing an entirely new layout of the home page. Standard templates let Booking.com deliv- ery teams set up tests with minimal effort, with processes such as user recruitment, randomization, recording visitors' behavior, and reporting entirely automated.[5]

The experiment results inform the product team's work and let the team draw its own road map using data rather than opinions. The team can make high-quality decisions in autonomy, without having to wait for validation from senior managers.

Experimentation Against Bureaucracy

The power of a strong experimentation culture goes beyond supporting teams in making better decisions. It reduces politics, because the empiri- cal data it generates helps convince everyone of which ideas are good for the customer rather than engage in wasteful debates based on opinions. As Scott Cook, the founder of Quicken and Intuit, put it:

> When you have only [run] one test, you don't have entrepre- neurs, you have politicians, because you have to sell. Out of a hundred good ideas, you've got to sell your idea. So you build up a society of politicians and salespeople. When you have five hundred tests you're running, then everybody's ideas can run. And then you create entrepreneurs who run and learn and can retest and relearn as opposed to a society of politicians.[6]

A strong experimentation culture also facilitates collaboration across the organization. In his book *Scaling Teams*, David Loftesness gives an example of his own experience at Amazon, when he led the Search Relevance team at A9, an Amazon subsidiary focused on search technology. When the Personalization team at Amazon HQ came up with its own ideas on how to improve search result ranking, David and his team felt frustrated. They didn't like having another team making changes to their feature, especially when this required extra effort to coordinate launches and fix bugs.

Experiments run using Amazon's Weblab quickly settled the debate. Adding personalized recommendations along the search results created clear benefits to the bottom line. The Search Relevance team integrated the Personalization team's ideas into the core Amazon search infrastructure.[7] Easy experimentation turned what could have quickly become a turf war in a large bureaucracy into a flexible, fruitful collaboration instead, one that increased the value of the product for both the organization and its customers.

These examples from Booking.com, Intuit, and Amazon have one limitation in common: they all rely on experimentation platforms plugged onto their products. These experimentation platforms test incremental product changes, which limits learnings to the current product and doesn't help imagine what new products customers could need. To avoid focusing all the learnings around faster horses, how can we dive deeper into what would actually benefit customers, regardless of our existing capabilities and assets?

Develop Customer Empathy to Understand Which "Others" to Learn From

Problem solving and experimenting on the current products and services is a key first step in learning about the customer. To go further and learn more about what customers need than they know themselves, we must start from the customers and develop deep empathy around their problems and needs.

Identify Your Customer's "Job to Be Done" to Understand the Alternatives

Understanding the problems customers face is what Clayton Christensen calls understanding the "job to be done." When considering a particular customer problem, for example, going from A to B faster, understanding the "job to be done" is not about benchmarking against all the similar products offered by direct competitors, such as different breeds of horses. Rather, we benchmark against every alternative that the customer could consider when faced with the frustration that the product or service is meant to address. To understand all those alternatives, one needs to develop deep empathy with customers.

To illustrate how creative this can lead us to be, Christensen uses the example of a customer buying a milkshake on the way to work. The trap would be to benchmark against competitors' milkshakes and evaluate them using industry standards, such as price, chunkiness, chewiness, or chocolateness, reinforcing current beliefs in that industry.

To avoid this, we first must understand why morning commuters are buying the milkshake, or to use Christensen's concept, what job the milkshake is hired to do. After observing customers for a few days and interviewing some of them, it appeared that the morning commuters were hiring the milkshake to keep the long and boring commute interesting while addressing their midmorning hunger. For customers, alternatives are not other milkshakes, but anything from bananas to doughnuts, bagels, breakfast bars, or even coffee. The customer evaluates these alternatives by various metrics:

- Can I use the product while driving?
- Does it last for my whole car journey?
- Does it make my car or my hands messy?
- Does it fill me up for the whole morning?

Similarly, because Ford customers' "job to be done" was moving from A to B, Ford cars had two important advantages over horses: increased speed and reduced horse manure.

Think Customer First by "Working Backward" with Amazon's PR/FAQ

In our experience, developing the customer empathy that is required to effectively identify the "jobs to be done" calls for real effort. It is hard to go from building the solution, which requires a dive deep into details and thinking analytically about a multitude of practical problems, to putting oneself into the customer's shoes, which requires taking a huge step back to feel the customers' frustrations and understand all the alternatives they could consider.

We have found Amazon's PR/FAQ, short for Press Release/Frequently Asked Questions, very helpful in keeping the customer's point of view at the center of a team's discovery process.

PR/FAQ dates back to 2004, when Amazon launched its new digital media organization with Bill Carr at its helm. At first everyone thought the challenge would be just like any previous category expansion at Amazon: gather the data to build a catalog of items, establish relationships with vendors to source them, set prices, build content for category pages, and then launch the new business.

But after several meetings, it became obvious that Carr and his team were too deep into the financials and not focused enough on the customer. Bezos tried to help them by suggesting they create mock-ups to better visualize the customer experience. He asked how customers would read e-books. Would they work on tablet, phone, and PC? But the team postponed answering those questions precisely, arguing that it was better to launch the business first and think about those details later.

This convinced Bezos that they were not giving enough thought to the customer. Amazon's success was built on becoming Earth's most customer-centric company. How it would ensure a much better customer experience than what was already available was not a detail.

By putting the customer back at the center, the digital media team members realized that they were working on something very different from any other Amazon business. They could also see that their spreadsheet-and-slide approach was not helping them. It kept them focused on how they would build solutions, rather than on taking the necessary step back to think about what would make for a great customer experience.

After multiple iterations, Bezos came up with the idea of making the team write an imaginary press release about the ideal, yet-to-be-created customer experience. Not only did this format free the team members from Excel and PowerPoint, allowing them to think in the narrative form; it also helped them finally focus on what would be great for customers. This helped them realize that, when it came to digital content, customer's reading experience was still lacking. To create a truly unique customer experience, they needed a new, much better reading device. That's how the Kindle was born.

The Kindle was among the first Amazon products that benefited from this new imaginary press release approach, which became known as the PR/FAQ. Bill Carr credits it for helping his team clarify that the e-book store needed to be deeply integrated with the reading device, which required creating an in-house hardware capability. That seemed crazy at the time, considering Amazon's total lack of expertise in the domain. It also helped the team come up with two of the key features that made the Kindle great at its launch: Whispernet, an always-on 3G connection to buy new books from anywhere in less than 60 seconds, and the e-ink screen technology that made for an excellent reading experience.

PR/FAQ put the members of the team in their customers' shoes. The resulting empathy let them benchmark the customer experience they wanted to build against the alternatives their customers already used. They were not comparing the Kindle with other e-readers, but with the centuries-old printed book. This explains why they adopted the e-ink technology. Despite its slow refresh rate, it made the Kindle reading experience remarkably similar to paper and much more comfortable than devices that used traditional screens. Readers could use a Kindle screen in the sun by the pool without experiencing any glare, for example. Its lower energy consumption also allowed customers to use it on a long-haul flight without worrying about the battery. Making the reading experience close to that of reading a book also explains why the team spent a lot of time fine-tuning the weight and shape of the Kindle, to ensure the reading experience was comfortable over a long period of time. PR/FAQ helped the team clarify their customers' "job to be done" and come up with a new and better experience to address that need.

Customer-Centric Learning

Building a successful learning organization is not just about encouraging people in the organization to learn. For it to be sustainable, it needs to contribute to value for the customer, which is why we need to start by learning what customers need. To create a customer-centric learning culture, we first focus on the customers' current frustrations and address them with systematic problem solving. We then use continuous product experimentation to learn about what could improve the current customer experience. Finally, to make sure we don't limit our learnings to existing products, we develop deep customer empathy, understanding our customers' job to be done. This creates a culture where teams understand customers much better and can more easily come up with new ways to create and deliver them value.

A challenge at scale, however, is making sure that the organization doesn't keep on reinventing the wheel, whether because new people join or because we don't look enough at what's already been invented outside the organization. How can we make sure the organization remembers past learnings from both within and outside itself, and actually builds knowledge?

19

BUILD KNOWLEDGE

Keeping Teams Stable

The most direct way to retain knowledge is to keep teams stable for as long as possible. Research has consistently shown that spoken interpersonal communications, rather than written information, are the primary means by which engineers collect and transfer new ideas and information.[1] Three studies on the relationship between team tenure and performance (Pelz and Andrews, 1966; Smith, 1970; and Katz, 1982) have confirmed that team performance increases for the first one and a half years.[2]

The same studies also showed that performance started decreasing after five years, but in our fast-paced tech world, this is something we never had to worry about. On the contrary, we more commonly see teams assembled for just a few months to deliver a particular milestone or feature set, then disbanded once the job is done, thus losing all their accumulated knowledge.

Stable Product Team over Project-Based Planning

The approach of maintaining stable teams instead of building ad-hoc teams is what Marty Cagan calls "dedicated product teams," as opposed to "project-based planning"[3] or what Amazon calls "single-threaded teams."

These ongoing teams are given ownership of one area of the business and its corresponding objectives. Team members stay for more than a year, not just the few weeks or months required to complete a specific project. Stability allows the team to both grow its domain experience and develop enough trust among team members to challenge each other. This quickly translates into higher velocity, better product quality, and enough accumulated deep expertise to come up with the real innovations that most affect business outcomes.

Products Versus Tools

It is not incompatible to have dedicated product teams and to deliver a variety of projects. A dedicated product team can deliver different projects, provided the flow of projects stays within the stable domain that it is responsible for and growing expertise in. The team should also be in charge of maintaining the mature systems that are part of that domain.

Conversely, if a mature system isn't part of an active product domain and does not benefit from continuous improvement, it is officially legacy. This should be limited to systems that are not core to the business and in which maintaining deep expertise and continuous improvement does not bring enough business value to be worthwhile.

This is not the distinction we see in many corporate IT departments, where the "plan, build, run" mindset means that every product goes to maintenance teams as soon as the build teams have finished their work. This effectively means pushing every new product into the legacy category as soon as it is released, discarding the experience that the build teams have accumulated on that product and that they could leverage to continue improving it over many more years.

Creating Written Standards

That said, keeping teams stable can't be the only strategy for retaining knowledge, especially in a fast-growing environment. New people join, and new challenges need to be addressed. To build knowledge even when teams change, we can take advantage of a 5,000-year-old technology: the written form.

Work Is When People Don't Follow the Process

To better capture learnings in writing, we need to understand writing's limitations. In particular, we must dispel the illusion that we can perfectly document processes, because reality rarely follows the process. Work psychiatrist Christophe Dejours captures this idea well when he defines work as "the part of the job that is outside the process." To him, work starts the moment reality acts unexpectedly and the person in charge of a task adapts the process to that new reality.

Computers and robots mean that we can program perfectly predictable jobs, making this definition more relevant than ever. Human work is for all other cases: jobs that are too complex to program, where we need the ability to take initiative and adapt the process to a complex reality.

If a documented process can't take into account the whole reality of human work, what is the right way to document learnings?

The Standard: A Training Document on the Best Way to Do the Work

Lean thinking teaches us to create standards for documenting how work can be done. Standards are documents in which a team records what it thinks are the best ways to do something, observed within the team. The goal is not to create a process that teams must follow, but to create reference material for the existing team and training material for newcomers. Standards are guidelines that should not be followed blindly, but that everyone should be trained on before they set off to do the work and be encouraged to continuously improve.

Theodo standards include "How to easily get rid of circular dependencies in TypeScript," "How to run an efficient DynamoDB query," and "How to write a perfect User Story."

What Makes a Good Standard?

Lean standard format derives from a program called Training Within Industry (TWI), led by the U.S. Department of War during World War II. TWI was created to "win the war of production" by creating efficient training methods that would ensure the fast ramp-up of American military production. After the war, these effective methods were exported to Japan to help with the country's reconstruction. In the United States, however, they faded away with the shutdown of the U.S. government program and were only rediscovered decades later with the popularization of Lean thinking.[4]

A standard has two distinct parts. The first describes what "good" looks like and the second describes the job breakdown currently known to yield a good result.

These two distinct parts are important because they separate the definition of good quality, which is usually fairly consensual and stable over time, from the breakdown of one way to achieve it. That latter should be improved continuously as teams discover safer, more reliable, or faster ways to achieve the desired outcome.

Breaking down the job consists of identifying all the key steps at which one has to make a judgment call and for which there is a way to check the results. The job breakdown is traditionally displayed as a three-column table. Each row represents a key step in the process. The first column describes the key step, the second specifies how to check the results, ideally quantitatively, and the third gives examples or more background to explain the key step's relevance and importance.

Example of a Standard

How to Name Variables

What is a good variable name? (See Table 19.1.)

- Anyone on the team, including nontech domain experts, understands what it means without effort.
- The same concept is named consistently throughout the code.

TABLE 19.1   How to Name Variables

KEY STEPS	CHECK	EXAMPLES
Find the name domain experts would use to describe the concept.	The name can be used without confusion in a conversation with domain experts.	Don't use "purchase" if the domain experts only talk about "orders." Creating a common language between business and tech facilitates collaboration.
Choose a variable name that designates what the variable contains in plain English, as close as possible to the domain name.	Whole words Correct English Explicit about content	"employeeId" not "id"
Check whether the concept goes by a different name somewhere else in the code. Use the different name or refactor it into your version if it's worth the effort.	Only one name per concept throughout the code	"isOnlineOrder" and "isWebOrder" => Choose one and stick to it

How Should We Use and Maintain Standards?

It can be challenging to make sure standards are used at the right time and updated to keep up with any new knowledge the team generates. For this to happen, they must be embedded in the systematic problem solving.

Every time problem solving helps identify one or more root causes, leverage the following decision tree to use and update standards:

- For each root cause, is there a related standard?
  - **No.** If the root-cause is common enough, create a new standard.
  - **Yes.** Was the person who caused the problem trained on the standard?
    - **No.** An opportunity for training.
    - **Yes.** An opportunity to improve the standard to avoid similar misunderstandings in the future.

Over time this creates a strong and unique knowledge base that everyone in the organization can rely on. Of course, this knowledge building is all the more valuable if it builds atop the existing state of the art. How can a large organization, busy dealing with its own issues, find the energy to also look outside itself for learnings?

Learning from Others

Procter & Gamble's Successful Investment in Learning from Others

For generations, much of the phenomenal growth of Procter & Gamble (P&G) was a result of innovating from within: building global research facilities and hiring and holding onto the best talent in the world. That worked well while the world was less competitive and the company was smaller, up to "only" $25 billion in revenue.

However, by 2000 P&G was a $70 billion company with an annual organic growth of 4 to 6 percent, the equivalent of building a new $4 billion business every year. Generating such growth within the existing P&G innovation model of "invent it ourselves" was quickly becoming impossible. R&D productivity and innovation success rate—the percentage of new products that meet financial objectives—were both stagnating. This became visible in the first quarter of 2000, when flattening sales, lackluster new launches, and a quarterly earnings miss resulted in P&G losing half its market cap in just three months.

This was a wake-up call for the CEO, Alan Lafley. He asked the R&D department to broaden its horizon by looking at external sources of innovation. He gave the department the ambitious goal of acquiring 50 percent of future innovations from outside the company. Comparing the number of scientists worldwide working on similar topics with those of the 7,500 people in the R&D department, they realized that the 1.5 million people outside the organization probably had relevant research and ideas. This moved the company's negative attitude toward ideas "not invented here" toward enthusiasm for ideas "proudly found elsewhere."[5, 6]

By partnering with and learning from smaller companies, university and government labs, and even individuals eager to license and sell their intellectual property, P&G discovered the power of open innovation. As a result of this shift, by 2006 P&G reported an increase of nearly 60 percent in R&D productivity and the doubling of its innovation success rate. It reduced its R&D investment from 4.8 percent of sales in 2000 to 3.4 percent in 2006. Its share price went back to its precollapse heights.

Learn from Others with Benchmarking

To make learning from others systematic in an organization, we must create a practice of benchmarking. This can be found at Amazon, included in one of its leadership principles: "[Leaders] benchmark themselves and their teams against the best." It is also very prominent in Toyota's culture.

Toyota's Benchmarking Culture

In *Notes from Toyota-land: An American Engineer in Japan*,[7] Darius Mehri shares a story from his work in the engineering department of a Toyota Motor Group company between 1996 and 1999. His team was assigned the task of designing a new drag reducer from scratch. This was a challenging project with tight deadlines, but also an exciting undertaking for his engineering team. It was the first time in a long time that the team was starting from a blank canvas. Everyone was asked to offer proposals. Mehri dusted off his university textbooks on fluid mechanics, going back to first principles to work out some equations to inspire his design proposals.

In the meantime, his Japanese colleagues did something completely different. When it was time to present the proposals, the Japanese colleagues brought a large cardboard poster showing pictures of all the drag-reducing products currently used in the industry. They had even created models of each product and analyzed their respective merits using computational fluid dynamics software. In the words of Mehri: "Large, excruciatingly detailed charts filled the walls, comparing efficiency, gas mileage and other indicators. All the relevant parts had been cut up and placed on a table for us to examine. Each part was compared with the corresponding part from the competition's products."

Thanks to this benchmarking exercise, the team not only learned everything it needed to know about the competition's products, but also documented and filed the information on the intranet so any other engineer in the company could have immediate access to these learnings. Mehri quickly realized that this benchmarking practice was not specific to that team, but useful at all levels of product development: R&D, product design, and market analysis. It accelerated the design process and clarified what "best" looked like outside the organization.

The Risks of Benchmarking

Despite its obvious benefits, benchmarking is not that widespread, perhaps because it is a double-edged sword. If the benchmark scope is badly chosen, it can not only make learning ineffective, but actually lead to an excessive focus on misguided correlations that reinforce wrong beliefs.

Jerker Denrell, professor of behavioral science at the Warwick Business School, identifies three likely benchmarking mistakes: overvaluing risky practices, overvaluing self-reinforcing performance, and misinterpreting reverse causality. He gives a good example of the first and most prevalent mistake, which he identified in a study on diversity and innovation by Lee Fleming.

Fleming decided to test the common trope that diverse teams, composed of members from different disciplines, are more innovative. He analyzed the financial value of 17,000 patents[8] and realized that if you only consider successful patents and high-value innovations, diverse teams did seem to fare better. But when you include failures, things changed. While more-diverse teams had produced more of the rare breakthroughs, less-diverse teams had produced more value on average.

This is a good example of how benchmarking on the wrong subset of reality can lead to the wrong conclusion. To avoid this selection bias, we must make sure we look at the entire problem we are trying to address, not at a biased subset. This is why understanding what customers need and defining the "job to be done" accordingly is so critical in framing the study correctly.

Building Knowledge in a Fast-Changing World

What we frequently see in organizations is a regular inclination to come up with new ways of doing things on the fly, rather than leveraging current knowledge and expertise. To avoid reinventing the wheel, we need to build on past learnings. While keeping teams stable is the most straightforward way to ensure knowledge on a particular domain is retained over time, capturing some of these learnings in writing is necessary to transfer knowledge between teams and to newcomers.

Building on past learnings also includes looking outside the organization to study the current state of the art. Benchmarking is a powerful tool for this when used smartly while avoiding cognitive pitfalls.

One danger of building knowledge in our fast-changing industry, where the state-of-the-art constantly evolves, is to create a false feeling of expertise and not realize how fast past learnings are becoming obsolete. How can we make challenging "the way it's done here" a habit, to regularly refresh standards and make sure we keep building on the latest state of the art?

REFRESH KNOWLEDGE WITH KAIZEN

Make Innovation a Habit with Kaizen Workshops

To innovate, research says that a team needs both a structure and a focus on a creative objective,[1] to come up with genuinely new ideas and avoid what psychologists call the path of least resistance: going for the first intuition that comes to mind.[2] Lean thinking gives us a general-purpose framework that provides both of those: the six-step kaizen.

A General-Purpose Framework for Innovating

Kaizen is a Japanese word for "continuous improvement." Lean culture uses this concept to describe striving for small improvements, usually identified through quick experimentation. The six-step kaizen is one way to do kaizen, providing a framework to help teams apply the scientific method in a creative way to any challenge they might face.

At Theodo, we have successfully used kaizen to create a regular space for experimentation and innovation, where teams can take a step back from daily work. To help the team focus on a particular challenge without distraction, we usually run one-day workshops that we call "kaizen days." We aim to have one or two every week.

Kaizen workshops are led by an internal kaizen expert, chosen for having a good understanding of the group and a passion for both Lean and technology. These leaders can understand enough of the work's technical aspects to help the team focus on the right topics and reach the ambition level achievable in a day. Kaizen workshops are planned two weeks in advance, together with the team leader. The goal is to identify an interesting problem to examine and improve.

The Six-Step Kaizen Format

To share the learnings of the kaizen with the rest of the organization, we present them using a six-step structure:

1. Discover the improvement potential.
2. Analyze the current method.
3. Generate original ideas and choose one.
4. Develop a test plan.
5. Implement the plan.
6. Evaluate the new method.

We will address the theory before giving an example of a six-step kaizen at Theodo.

Step 1—Discover the Improvement Potential

This first step's goal is to determine a significant area of improvement for the team's activities. We usually focus on an operational problem that is relatively local and specific.

A good "improvement potential" is:

- A measurable objective, to run experiments rationally
- Impactful for customers, directly or indirectly

- Specific enough to allow for easy experiments
- A target ambitious enough to stretch the team's creativity and achievable enough to let people learn—aim for twice better or half as bad

Recognizing a reasonable target calls for a sense of what "good" looks like. This is knowledge that the kaizen expert can bring, leveraging the experience of coaching multiple kaizens. The team should also be curious and look at what outside best-in-class teams do. For example, improving the developers' working environment is a good way to start a kaizen session, and Tim Cochran's developer effectiveness reference table is a good starting point for looking at best in class (see Table 20.1).[3]

TABLE 20.1   Tim Cochran's Developer Effectiveness Reference Table

FEEDBACK LOOP	LOW EFFECTIVENESS	HIGH EFFECTIVENESS
Validate that a local code change works	2 mins	5–15 seconds (depending on tech choice)
Find root case for defect	4–7 days	1 day
Validate that a component integrates with other components	3 days to 2 weeks	2 hours
Validate that a change meets nonfunctional requirements	3 months	1 day to 1 week (depending on scope of change)
Become productive on a new team	2 months	4 weeks
Get answers to an internal technical query	1–2 weeks	30 mins
Launch a new service in production	2–4 months	3 days
Validate that a change was useful to the customer	6 months or more	1–4 weeks (depending on scope of change)

When choosing a potential improvement, avoid common mistakes:

- Don't address issues that are (or should be) in the backlog of the team's daily work. We take the team out of its usual environment for a reason: to take a step back and find new ways of creating value, not just to make progress on the backlog.
- Stay away from looking only at the process, and dive as much as possible into the technicalities of how value is created. The process can be improved during regular problem-solving sessions, whereas kaizen is about developing curiosity on how the team creates value. It aims to innovate around the craft and deepen expertise.

Once you've identified potential improvement, it is important to make it visual. This means:

- Measuring the current situation and collecting some historical data if possible, to visualize the trend
- Plotting the historical data and the objective on a graph, to make the improvement potential immediately visible to every participant

A word of caution if the measure is unstable: the true potential is the best repeatable result. Work as much on stabilizing the situation as on improving the average.

Step 2—Analyze the Current Method

The next step is to understand and analyze the current situation. For that, we recommend mapping the value flow to identify key steps and locate waste sources along the flow. Then break down all the possible factors that could affect the improvement potential.

We recommend finding at least seven factors, to exercise creativity and avoid rushing toward the first solution that comes to mind.

This is the step where we can also invest in building the workbench, to measure the situation more precisely. A recent example: a developer at Theodo built a puppeteer script to interact with a React form, to be able to repeat 10 times the measurement of "Total Blocking Time" and compute average and standard deviation automatically. This let the team members just run the script quickly during the rest of the day, to confirm whether they were improving the situation or not.

Step 3—Generate Original Ideas and Choose One

The goal is to generate new ideas about how we can address the problem and choose the one we want to implement now. Team members are free to express their imaginations. Write down every idea, even those that sound dumb. Quantity encourages divergent thinking, the ability to connect new information, ideas, and concepts that are usually far from one another. This is key in helping the team come up with completely new ideas. Later discussing why some ideas are not worth selecting will also generate valuable knowledge.

Once you have a list of about 10 ideas, choose the ones that stand out as a team. For those you select, think about quick tests that could test their potential. Run these quick tests, and using the results, select the one idea on which you want to focus the rest of the six-step kaizen.

Step 4—Develop a Test Plan

Don't jump straight into implementing the idea. First think about the consequences of implementing it. Almost every change to a system has consequences elsewhere, but in the middle of the euphoria of implementing a good idea, we often forget about the trade-offs. This is the time to take a step back and think hard about the side effects.

On the technical side, use the 3S quality framework:

- **Stability.** Have we forgotten any parts of the system that are closely tied to the part we plan to change? Could the change generate bugs there or anywhere else?
- **Speed.** Will the change affect performance or scalability? Will the database be able to cope with it?

- **Security.** Does the change open a back door by mistake? Are we publishing information we should not?

On the organization and the people sides, the team should consider other questions: Whom does the plan affect? Whom should we convince before going forward with our change? How will we convince them? These questions help us reflect on what is actually needed to make change happen, which develops leadership among team members and fosters cooperation, a nice side effect of kaizen.

Don't move forward until you have defined how you will measure your experiment's success (or failure). Without a good check in place, there can be no validated learning.

Step 5—Implement the Plan

Implement the change everywhere it can be implemented. Typically, when we change a piece of code in a large software system, we can easily forget to update spots where a very similar piece of code exists. Not implementing the change everywhere is a big source of future defects, something you should strive to avoid.

Do not forget to keep a record of the change (e.g., the code diff) to document it in your kaizen six-step report.

Step 6—Evaluate the New Method

In Step 4, we insisted on the importance of a clear definition of the experiment's success. In Step 6, we use that definition to measure the effects of the change.

Did the change have no positive effect? Or worse, did it have unintended negative side effects? If the answer is "yes," it is still good news. The team will have learned a lot by comparing intuition with reality and will remember the lesson. In this case, revert to the initial state. This is an important opportunity for leaders to recognize people for their efforts and learnings, not the results. Think like Thomas Edison. After five months spent on developing a nickel-iron battery, his associate challenged him on his lack of results. His reply was: "Results! Why, man, I have gotten a lot of results! I know several thousand things that won't work."

By identifying our misconceptions, even if it's through thousands of failures, we better understand how things work and are able to make better decisions in the future.

Similarly, if the change turns out to be positive, we should still direct recognition first to efforts and learnings, rather than to the results themselves. The priority in kaizen is that the team learns about its work and slowly becomes more confident in experimenting with new methods.

If the implemented change is successful, the team should document it and share it with the rest of the organization. This is what Lean calls "standardize and share." We will address later how to document such new learnings using "standards" and how to share them effectively throughout the organization.

Over the course of the experiment, the team probably saw a lot of other potential improvement opportunities. Leverage that by planning the next kaizen session right away.

EXAMPLE OF A KAIZEN DAY

Reduce Hot Reload of the NestJS Server on a Project from 10.7s to 4.7s

Step 1—Discover the Improvement Potential

Software engineers regularly check how code changes have affected an app. The standard method is to stop the app, recompile the code, and restart the app. This process can take minutes, not seconds, and can make software engineers' work tedious during development, particularly when they're iterating quickly on small changes, such as testing different layouts in a user interface to decide which one feels best. To avoid the wait, some frameworks offer a "hot-reload" option, which lets engineers swap new code for old without stopping and restarting the app, and with minimal recompiling.

In this example, the team is working on a backend API written in TypeScript using a framework called NestJS. NestJS offers the hot-reload capability, so the API results should display any change to the backend JavaScript code in a matter of seconds. But there is very big improvement potential: What should feel real time (less than 2 seconds) is actually taking 10.7 seconds at every change (see Figure 20.1).

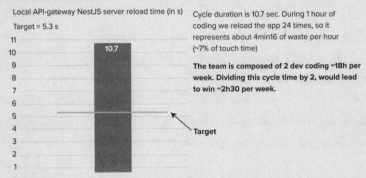

Local API-gateway NestJS server reload time (in s)

Target = 5.3 s

Cycle duration is 10.7 sec. During 1 hour of coding we reload the app 24 times, so it represents about 4min16 of waste per hour (~7% of touch time)

The team is composed of 2 dev coding ~18h per week. Dividing this cycle time by 2, would lead to win ~2h30 per week.

10.7

Target

FIGURE 20.1   Illustrating the improvement potential in Step 1 of a six-step kaizen.

The team measures how often teams use hot reload; the answer is about 24 times an hour, which means 2 hours wasted per week. The goal is to halve that hot-reload time to save an hour a week. Saved time is a benefit, and so is the improvement to the working conditions, as having to wait more than 10 seconds after every code change to check the impact doesn't allow developers to iterate fast and stay in the flow.

Step 2—Analyze the Current Method

The team takes multiple measurements to observe the variations in hot-reload time, and breaks down the total time in substeps (see Table 20.2).

TABLE 20.2 Measurements in Step 2 of a Six-Step Kaizen

	1	2	3	4	5	6	7	8	9	10
Webpack(s)	7.1	7.5	7.1	7.6	7.3	7.7	7.7	7.4	7.4	7.9
Error(s)	2	2	2	2	2	2	2	1.6	1.9	2
Nest Start(s)	2	1.2	1.7	1.5	1.2	1.2	1.2	1.2	1.4	1.3
Total(s)	11.1	10.7	10.8	11.1	10.5	10.9	10.9	10.2	10.7	11.2

	MEDIAN	STANDARD DEVIATION	MIN
Webpack(s)	7.45	0.26	7.1
Error(s)	2	0.13	1.6
Nest Start(s)	1.25	0.27	1.2
Total(s)	10.7	0.40	9.9

The team analyzes what happens during hot reload and maps the system to get a better shared understanding of the current situation.

Step 3—Generate Original Ideas and Choose One

This lets the team members come up with multiple improvement ideas, which they list and score, based on effect and cost (see Table 20.3).

TABLE 20.3   Measurements in Step 3 of a Six-Step Kaizen

IDEA	IMPACT	COST	COMMENT
Correct the server disconnect error wasting 2s	Average	High	Next kaizen
Test a route using integration tests instead of Swagger	Average	High	Better feedback loop
Hot reload instead of live reload	?	High	Read doc
Reduce compile time in Webpack	High	High	No idea how to start
Change compiler	?	High	SWC not yet compatible with Nest
Use cache to recompile only modified files	High	Low	OK

One idea stands out: "Use cache to recompile only modified files."

Step 4—Develop a Test Plan

The team thinks about the change's likely impact. In this case, any side effects would be limited and there is no need to train the team. The only caution is that the team must warn the ops team in the very unlikely event of cache issues occurring in production.

Step 5—Implement the Plan

The plan is to enable the cache in Webpack, a tool used to bundle all the code together before the NestJS server sends it to the user. The cache will save a lot of time by only recompiling modified files.

The team realizes it must change just one line in Webpack's configuration code to make this happen. A whole kaizen for one line of code might feel like overkill, but this is actually a sign that we have discovered a bug in the tooling. Webpack always recompiles all files, which isn't consistent with hot reload. The documentation confirms it: cache should be the default behavior in development mode, and there should be no need to set that default explicitly in the configuration file. The team has discovered an interesting misconception here. It learned it trusted its open-source tooling a bit too much and probably wasted time looking for the problem in the wrong places.

The team documents the change by taking a screenshot of the code change. It also adds a thorough comment directly in the code, to help future code readers understand the importance of that single line.

Step 6—Evaluate the New Method

The team measures the improvement and finds that it has reached the target of cutting recompiling time in half (see Figure 20.2). It shares learnings with the internal NestJS guild and further explores why it had to enforce default behavior in the configuration file. The team finds a bug in NestJS and contributes the fix to the open-source project.

The team soon does another kaizen on a "server disconnect" error, which brings the hot-reload time from 4.7 seconds to 2.8 seconds and brings new learnings on the subtleties of NestJS's database connection layer, greatly improving the team's expertise on the topic.

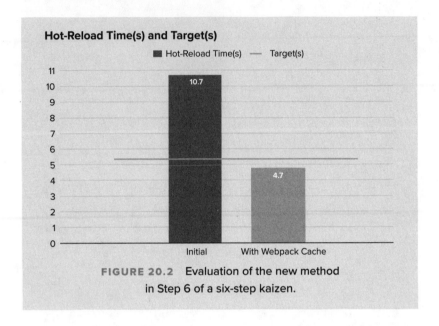

Hot-Reload Time(s) and Target(s)

■ Hot-Reload Time(s)   — Target(s)

FIGURE 20.2   Evaluation of the new method
in Step 6 of a six-step kaizen.

To build superior stability, performance, and security in digital products, software engineers need a deep understanding of the systems on which their products are built. But as the development ecosystem matures, there are more and more layers of technology built to abstract the lower-level systems and facilitate development. While these abstractions help developers work faster, they prevent them from deepening their understanding of the whole system. Kaizen provides an opportunity to explore how things work at lower levels, helping developers acquire the same deep expertise as their more experienced peers who learned their trade when there were fewer abstractions.

A General-Purpose Framework to Keep Improving Knowledge

Regular kaizen gives us an opportunity to refresh our standards and challenge our beliefs by providing a framework to help the organization regularly take a step back from daily work.

Kaizen helps the team members look deep into their craft and think creatively about how to create significantly more value. After a kaizen session, they will have seen how the current standard is lacking and have the opportunity to refresh it. They will also have improved the mastery of their craft and developed deeper expertise.

Now that we have more confidence that learnings will be refreshed and improved regularly with kaizen, how can we spread them across the organization?

21

SPREAD THE LEARNINGS THROUGHOUT THE ORGANIZATION

Give Everyone Access to All the Information

When American computer programmer and coauthor of the Manifesto for Agile Software Development Ward Cunningham launched WikiWikiWeb, the first user-editable website in 1995, he transformed the way we share information. He was probably unaware at the time of the impact his invention would have, but 25 years later, its technology powers Wikipedia, the biggest encyclopedia in recorded history with more than 59 million articles, around 2 billion unique device visits per month, and more than 17 million monthly edits.

Wikis and the more modern equivalents such as Confluence or Notion are now also present in every company, replacing what used to be hundreds of binders that made it difficult to spread knowledge around. In a tech organization, this is where standards typically reside, allowing anyone to access shared learnings and contribute when a problem-solving or kaizen activity highlights the need to improve the standard.

A limitation of wikis and intranets, however, is that learnings are mostly shared to those actively looking for them. To address this we can leverage Obeyas and data platforms.

Visual Sharing of Information with Obeyas

Nine Lies About Work offers an example of how sharing learnings more widely can create powerful collective intelligence. The authors describe the Royal Air Force war room's key role in the Battle of Britain:

> In late 1940, Hitler's armies had swept across Europe to the shores of France, and Britain's Royal Air Force was all that stood between them and the conquest of the British Isles. Although the RAF had been able to increase the number of fighter aircraft available over the course of the summer months, what it had was still not enough. [. . .] What the RAF needed, if the country were to be saved, was a force multiplier—something that made their limited roster of planes and pilots vastly more effective. The force multiplier they came up with was a room.

The room was used to visualize all the information available: the status of each plane, how long each had been airborne, the number of pilots available, the position of barrage balloons, and the position of all observed planes, whether friend or foe:

> What the room does is bring together all of these data points in real time and then present them so that frontline team members—called controllers—can exercise their judgment and can send their forces to where they know the enemy is. [. . .] It was a force multiplier that increased average interception rates from the pre-war level of between 30 percent and 50 percent to an average of 90 percent, and often 100 percent, which is to say it doubled the effectiveness of the defending force.[1]

This is not a reporting system in which data is collected for an organization's leaders. It's one that gives everyone quick and easy access to the big picture, giving them a full perspective before they make decisions. "This kind of perspective was once limited to senior leaders," says General McChrystal in his book *Team of Teams*, explaining information sharing during the war in Iraq. "In the old model, subordinates provided information and leaders disseminated commands. We reversed it: We had our leaders provide information so that subordinates, armed with context, understanding, and connectivity, could take the initiative and make decisions."[2]

Compared with just sharing learnings on an intranet, a situation room makes it easy for everyone in the organization to regularly see all the learnings. It provides a global overview of the systems involved and is a place for different teams working together to have data-informed conversations.

This is the role of the Obeya, which we talked about in Part Two: "Lead with Value for the Customer." All the learnings are displayed across the walls of the "large room" and shared with every project contributor. People can see the bigger picture and decide which learnings are most relevant to their own context.

The learnings should include a list of important "known unknowns": the challenges that the organization must tackle, despite having no idea how it will do that. This is an important way to tap collective intelligence and find new solutions.

Take for example Google founder Larry Page in 2002. On a Friday evening he posted results from Google's AdWords engine on the office kitchen walls. Across the top, he wrote "THESE ADS SUCK."[3] What he lacked in politenesss he made up for in broad communication of a challenge that the organization needed to tackle. By early Monday morning, a group of engineers had sent out an email with a solution that resolved the AdWords problem and contributed to Google's growth.

An Obeya efficiently shares learnings among people and stimulates their creativity. But there's a trade-off: information on an Obeya's wall can't be used directly by software. To multiply our data's leverage, we would need the machine equivalent of an Obeya.

Self-Service Intelligence with the Right Data Platform

In our tech economy, large sets of structured data have become a key source of value, especially with the rise of AI. Software creates and stores data about customers and business that when aggregated and shared across silos, generates invaluable intelligence.

Just as an Obeya shares learnings with everyone in the organization, we need a machine equivalent to share data across organizational systems, with self-service access. To guarantee self-service access is easier said than done, but with software moving to the cloud and good-quality APIs, it is becoming more and more attainable.

Technology is evolving too fast for us to give specific recommendations. That said, the typical data architecture has been stable for a while now. Interestingly, good data architecture looks very similar to the U.S. Joint Force Command model for Intelligence.[4] (See Figure 21.1.)

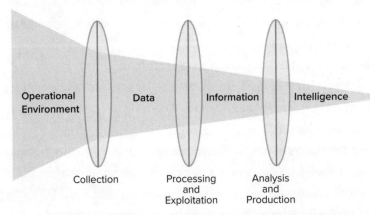

FIGURE 21.1   Relationship of data, information, and intelligence.
Source: Joint Intelligence/Joint Publication 2.0 (Joint Chiefs of Staff)

Both architecture and model entail collecting data from the operational environment. In a tech organization, this requires ensuring that every data source is accessible, at least through a self-service API that lets users pull out information at regular intervals. It is even better to have an event system that pushes data as soon as it's created or updated, enabling real-time integration with the rest of the information system.

Next, both data architecture and the Joint Chiefs of Staff model process the data to create information. This is often the role of the data warehouse, which brings together all the data and combines it for easy access.

Finally, both share an analysis phase, leveraging the expertise of people in the business to identify signals that matter and turn information into intelligence. This is typically the realm of complex queries and data visualization platforms.

It's important to remember that an Obeya should be an intelligence system, not a reporting system. Data should be as widely accessible as possible, both through self-service APIs and on the data visualization platform.

Develop Effective Training Programs

While leveraging Obeyas and data platforms helps share information more widely, it doesn't replace proper training when it comes to transferring the experience and intuition that turn information into knowledge. Let's look at how to create training programs that do this effectively.

Productive Training Sessions

Earlier we introduced Training Within Industry (TWI) when explaining standards. TWI also provides a strong approach to training. The TWI motto is simple: if the student hasn't learned, it means the teacher hasn't taught. TWI puts responsibility for student learning squarely on the teacher.

TWI offers trainers a four-step method for effectively checking that trainees have learned:

1. Trainer explains the theory using the standard.
2. Trainer demonstrates and shows how the standard works.
3. Students try on their own while trainer observes.

4. Trainer gives feedback on student performance and for each mistake refers to the standard.

In our experience, most trainers who haven't learned this method miss the third and fourth steps. Asking students who just heard your explanation to demonstrate what they learned highlights the awkward difference between what you said and what they heard. This is exactly the point of the TWI method. It highlights misunderstandings so you can correct them swiftly. And students who see the misconceptions that were about to survive the training session are usually more receptive to personalized feedback from their teacher.

Tailored Training Schedules

When should training happen?

Ad-hoc Training Pulled by Problem Solving

The most relevant way to schedule training is to use problem solving as a trigger. Every time a problem-solving exercise highlights a skill gap, the team leader should schedule a one-on-one training session with the person who is struggling with the standard. This puts the need for teaching and the lesson very close together, maximizing the lesson's effectiveness.

Regular Training Pulled by the Skills Matrix

There are also many situations in which training can and should be scheduled in advance. Newcomers will need to be onboarded, and teams will predictably require certain expertise. An organization can anticipate which trainings are needed to support people in doing high-quality work.

The key is to clarify the current training situation compared with the anticipated needs by relying on a useful visual management tool known as a "skills matrix." A skills matrix usually takes the form of a row per person in the team and a column per skill that will be required in the near future. At the intersection of each row and column, we can then visualize each person's expertise in that particular skill.

The levels are traditionally represented using Harvey balls (Figure 21.2):

- Untrained
- Trained on the standard
- Can do with help
- Can do without help
- Can teach

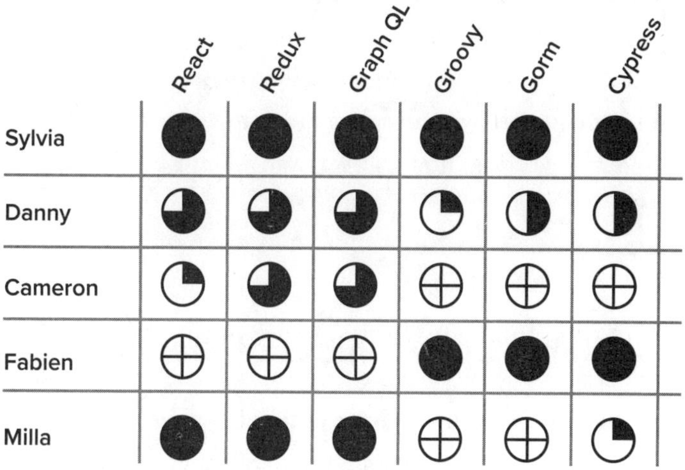

FIGURE 21.2   A skills matrix using Harvey balls.

Once the team can see who needs training on what, it can create a regular training schedule. That could be one-to-one training sessions with the team leader or more formal training programs.

Data-Driven Training

Data and AI offer a new way to identify training needs.

Amazon's Connections is a good example. It asks all 1.6 million Amazonians a question every day, when they log into their computer or workstation. It poses questions on a wide range of topics, from work environment to the manager's effectiveness, team dynamics, and (most important) any barriers getting in the way of employees inventing on behalf of customers.

Connections then aggregates the 1.5 million answers collected every day and shares them with managers, creating a culture of real-time feedback. It also uses an algorithm to analyze the data, identify improvement opportunities, and suggest to managers the relevant learning assets, such as online training, that can help them immediately improve.

Upskilling When There Is No Training

By leveraging standards, TWI, and smart ways to tailor training to individual needs, we can efficiently spread existing learnings throughout the organization. Of course, this supposes that these learnings and associated training materials exist. In a tech industry where the state of the art is continuously evolving, how can we train when no one can yet act as a teacher?

Enable Global Communities of Practice

Training on a topic without a teacher or training material is actually possible. We do it effectively through communities of practice, a concept popularized by Etienne Wenger's 1998 book *Communities of Practice*.

Communities of Practice

Communities of practice are groups of people who share a problem or a passion for an activity. They hope to improve their abilities through regular interaction.[5] These can be in person or online, and don't need to be formal. Learning happens through sharing experiences and knowledge in free-flowing, creative ways, without a predetermined goal.[6]

Benefits of Communities of Practice

A community of practice is not merely a community of interest—like an interest in certain kinds of movies, for instance. Members interact around their shared practice: experiences, stories, tools, ways of addressing recurring problems, and so on. These informal interactions help group members in different ways: joint problem solving, informal support, asset reuse, coordination, synergy creation, documentation, and awareness about different approaches to similar problems.[7] Communities generate learnings that eventually can be recorded in standards for more structured training later.

Xerox offers a good example of large-scale sharing of learnings through communities of practice. The company has 25,000 customer service representatives worldwide who are in charge of fixing Xerox printers when there is an issue at the client's site. Representatives learn quickly that these large machines, made up of multiple subsystems, are not particularly predictable. They're influenced by a wide range of factors: age, condition, use, and environment, which may be hot, cold, damp, dry, clean, dusty, secluded, in traffic, and so on. Documentation only goes so far in helping the representatives solve the problems they encounter. The difference between doing a cheap fix and replacing a $40,000 machine is often down to what a representative knows about similar, past situations.

When Xerox leadership tried to understand what made some groups of representatives perform better than others, they discovered one group's secret: its breakfast ritual. The group had set up an informal community of practice around breakfast. In between gossip, they shared tips and stories on how they dealt with new issues, helping each other overcome the most difficult problems.

Realizing the value of this knowledge-sharing practice, Xerox leadership deployed it globally by creating Eureka, an online platform to connect all the company's representatives around a shared database of tips. To maintain the spirit of the community of practice, they made sure the database contained only tips supplied and vetted by the representatives. It rewarded the best tips not with money, but with community recognition.

Xerox had a big success with Eureka. Representatives adopted it widely, and the global community of practice organized around the Eureka database saved the organization an estimated $100 million.

Enabling Communities of Practice

At Theodo, we have active communities of practice, which we call "guilds," on such topics as security, web performance, green IT, and accessibility. We have found factors that are key in growing communities of practice:

- Identify relevant domains of expertise. Look for areas in which knowledge sharing would be useful to the organization that are also exciting enough to attract a community. Good examples in tech might include security, web performance, and testing.
- For each domain of expertise, identify a passionate leader and support that person in gathering a group of enthusiastic early adopters.
- Provide a budget and infrastructure to fund and protect the community of practice. Intervene when the community runs up against obstacles to progress, such as promotion systems that overlook community contributions or reward structures that discourage collaboration.
- Promote the value of communities of practice by giving them visibility and sharing the best stories of collaboration and innovation they have enabled.

Promoting communities of practice does not have to be complicated. For example, at Theodo the security guild sends the whole organization a monthly newsletter that shares the guild's best learnings in a compelling and easily understood way. Not only does this increase awareness of our security challenges, but it also reminds everyone in the organization that this guild exists and does valuable work.

Building a Learning Organization to Create Value for the Customer

"Responding to change over following a plan" is probably the value in the Agile manifesto that most embodies what people expect from the methodology. After all, the original definition of "Agile" is the ability to move quickly.

Similarly, "Agile at scale" means a large organization able to move quickly in an ever-changing environment to follow its customers' changing needs and adapt by launching new products and services. This requires building a learning organization.

The Amazon example also shows how the four principles shared in this book form a complete system. The startup began as an online bookshop, but to scale its mission "to be Earth's most customer-centric company," it had to empower its people with a tech-enabled network of teams and pioneered devops excellence with practices similar to right-first-time and just-in-time. When it then followed its customers into new markets and realized that it could not rely solely on its existing knowledge and expertise, it built a learning organization. Beth Galetti, senior vice president of human resources at Amazon, describes it well:

> Our customers' needs evolve and grow, so continuous learning is an imperative for all Amazonians. We capture this intent in our leadership principle, "Learn and Be Curious." That principle is very important because we are frequently doing things that have never been done before. For this reason, there is often no playbook to teach nor experts to follow, so we empower people to try new things and learn along the way.[8]

Building a learning organization is probably the principle that best embodies Agile at scale. However, it works best when the organization is motivated by the North Star of delivering more value to the customer, and its people are both empowered and challenged to learn: empowered by the tech-enabled network of teams and challenged by the high delivery standards of right-first-time and just-in-time.

PART SEVEN

Conclusion

人22

A DIFFERENT PARADIGM

A Different Paradigm
to Scaling a Tech Organization

We decided to build a startup in 2007 to escape the corporate world. We were idealistic enough to believe we could be more ingenious than the bureaucracies we had observed and wanted to come up with something better. It took time to finally get there, but we had a first glimpse of hope when we went all-in on Agile in 2012. We were able to build better products, faster and cheaper, in a way that was more enjoyable both for our clients and for us.

When we started growing fast, however, we faced new challenges. Mastering Agile had not been easy, but at least we could refer to the manifesto. We had methodologies like Scrum and Extreme programming to train on and a vibrant community to connect with. The challenges of leading a fast-growing company were much more complex, and we couldn't find a recipe like Scrum that we could apply. The widespread consensus was that when an organization grows, the only solution is to put processes and hierarchies in place to ensure that workers do the right thing.

The existence of companies that didn't seem to follow this rule, including Amazon, Apple, and Tesla, inspired us to look for more ingenious ways of scaling Theodo. Thanks to some incredible opportunities to learn from experts in the Agile, devops, and Lean communities, we understood that these companies didn't take inspiration just from Agile, but also from Lean thinking. That led us to learn how to leverage it ourselves at Theodo.

Lean thinking helped us scale the company in a completely different way, just like Agile had given us a completely different way to consider how we would work as a team of software developers.

In Lean thinking:

- We gain market share not by competing on price, but by providing more value to the customer and society.
- We don't scale management by creating processes that people follow, but by empowering teams on standards they train on and improve.
- Our operations are more profitable, not because of cost-cutting but because of reduced waste during production, thanks to right-first-time and just-in-time.
- Innovation does not come from thinking in the boardroom, but from building a learning organization that tries to create more value for customers.

We progressively adapted this paradigm from its manufacturing origins to our tech industry, inspired by some of the best tech companies that had followed this path before us. We captured our learnings in the four guiding principles of the Lean Tech Manifesto. We hope the manifesto can help you adopt this alternative point of view in your own tech organization and succeed at scaling while maintaining an Agile culture.

A Different Paradigm for the Big Challenges of the Twenty-First Century

This different paradigm is not just a better way to scale an organization. We believe it is a better way to face the big challenges of the twenty-first century.

With technology evolving at an unprecedented rate and educational systems struggling, the education challenge is to adapt and stay relevant. Lean thinking teaches us how to embed a learning system within operations. This lets us build organizations where people benefit from continuous learning on the job and keep up with fast-paced innovation.

The future of work challenge, with people looking for meaning while companies are pushed to focus on short-term share prices. Lean thinking provides a framework that focuses on long-term value for the customer and society and strives to empower everyone in the organization to contribute to it. This lets us build organizations where people's work can contribute more meaningfully.

The AI challenge, with recent AI innovations promising to replace millions of jobs and redefining where humans will actually be needed. Lean thinking provides decades of wisdom with the principle of human-machine separation on how to deal with automation. Toyota has always been careful to make sure automation was at the service of people, working to get the best of both worlds: productivity and creativity. Not only is this more respectful of humans: it has also achieved better results than overautomation, a lesson Tesla learnt the hard way when it had to backtrack on its automation efforts. Human-machine separation gives us a model to build organizations where automation empowers humans, rather than enslaving them.

The sustainability challenge, in a world where companies can no longer ignore the external consequences of their growth. Everything in Lean thinking is about finding ingenious ways to reduce waste and do better with less, for the organization and society. Sustainability's challenge will not be solved by just a few technological breakthroughs. We will need collective intelligence to do better with less in many aspects of society. By building Lean organizations, we empower people to develop their ingenuity at the service of more sustainability.

These big challenges highlight the ways the current paradigm is failing us. Companies that don't care about the external consequences of their short-term thinking are rightly criticized. But trying to address the current challenges of society by adding an environmental, social, and governance (ESG) score to companies' annual reports is like putting a bandage on a wooden leg.

Leaders need a new way of thinking. Lean thinking is that paradigm shift, helping leaders lead differently and be better suited for the challenges we face as organizations and as a society.

By showing how Lean can benefit the new generation of tech companies, we hope this book will contribute to spreading this better, more ingenious paradigm across the industry.

NOTES

Our Journey

1. https://web.archive.org/web/20131217174707/http://www.controlchaos.com/storage/scrum-articles/Sutherland%20200111%20proof.pdf.
2. http://www.extremeprogramming.org/rules.html.

Chapter 1

1. https://spectrum.ieee.org/the-surprising-story-of-the-first-microprocessors.
2. https://agilemanifesto.org/history.html.
3. https://www2.deloitte.com/content/dam/Deloitte/global/Documents/About-Deloitte/central-europe/ce-global-human-capital-trends.pdf.
4. https://ronjeffries.com/xprog/articles/safe-good-but-not-good-enough/.
5. https://kenschwaber.wordpress.com/2013/08/06/unsafe-at-any-speed/.
6. https://www.slideshare.net/BerndSchiffer/comparing-ways-to-scale-agile-at-agile-product-and-project-manager-meetup/9-Shitty_Agile_For_Enterprises_Martin.
7. https://software.af.mil/wp-content/uploads/2019/12/CSO-MFR-on-Agile-Frameworks-12282019.pdf.
8. https://scaledagile.com/case_study/fitbit/.
9. https://www.smharter.com/blog/the-mixed-results-of-companies-scaling-agile-with-a-scaled-framework/.
10. https://kenschwaber.wordpress.com/2013/08/06/unsafe-at-any-speed/.
11. https://www.fastcompany.com/3028213/how-to-manage-your-startups-fast-growth.
12. https://martinfowler.com/articles/evodb.html.
13. https://www.martinfowler.com/ieeeSoftware/whoNeedsArchitect.pdf.
14. https://www.drdobbs.com/open-source/the-agile-manifesto/184414755.

Chapter 2

1. https://digital.ai/resource-center/analyst-reports/state-of-agile-report/.
2. Hirotaka Takeuchi, and Ikujiro Nonaka, "The New New Product Development Game," *Harvard Business Review*, January 1986.
3. https://www.scrum.org/resources/scrum-development-process.
4. https://www.washingtonpost.com/archive/business/1993/08/15/what-japan-taught-us-about-quality/271f2822-b70d-4491-b942-4954caa710f8/.

5. https://deming.org/speech-by-dr-deming-to-japanese-business-leaders-in-1950/.
6. https://www.leanblog.org/2014/04/great-steve-jobs-video-transcript-from-1990-on
-continuous-improvement/.
7. https://www.amazon.jobs/en/principles.
8. https://www.mckinsey.com/capabilities/operations/our-insights/when-toyota-met
-e-commerce-lean-at-amazon.
9. https://www.sec.gov/Archives/edgar/data/1018724/000119312509081096/dex991.htm.
10. https://www.mckinsey.com/capabilities/operations/our-insights/when-toyota-met
-e-commerce-lean-at-amazon.

Chapter 3
1. https://www.theguardian.com/politics/2000/aug/18/welfarereform.politicalnews.
2. https://www.jfsa.org.uk/uploads/5/4/3/1/54312921/full_report_on_the_cancelled_
dhss_card.pdf.
3. https://publications.parliament.uk/pa/cm199900/cmselect/cmpubacc/406/40603.htm.

Chapter 4
1. https://www.zdnet.com/article/microsoft-has-97-of-os-market-says-onestat-com/.
2. https://gs.statcounter.com/os-market-share/all/worldwide/2021.
3. https://www.bloomberg.com/news/features/2017-09-29/the-equifax-hack-has-all-the
-hallmarks-of-state-sponsored-pros.
4. https://www.csoonline.com/article/3444488/equifax-data-breach-faq-what-happened
-who-was-affected-what-was-the-impact.html.
5. https://www.csoonline.com/article/3411139/equifax-s-billion-dollar-data-breach
-disaster-will-it-change-executive-attitudes-toward-security.html.
6. https://developers.google.com/web/tools/lighthouse.
7. https://en.wikipedia.org/wiki/Apdex.
8. https://www.fastcompany.com/1836987/listen-steve-jobs-payoff-great-employee.
9. https://backstage.io/blog/2020/10/22/cost-insights-plugin.
10. https://aws.amazon.com/blogs/aws/new-customer-carbon-footprint-tool/.
11. https://cloud.google.com/carbon-footprint.

Chapter 5
1. Keynote: Making Progress—Alan Kay, https://youtu.be/9MqVfzxAp6A?t=960.
2. https://rework.withgoogle.com/print/guides/5721312655835136/.
3. https://rework.withgoogle.com/print/guides/5721312655835136/.
4. https://www.gallup.com/workplace/286997/ideal-team-size-depends-manager.aspx.
5. https://en.wikipedia.org/wiki/Matrix_management.
6. https://hbr.org/1990/07/matrix-management-not-a-structure-a-frame-of-mind.
7. https://hbr.org/2020/11/how-apple-is-organized-for-innovation.
8. https://www.lean.org/the-lean-post/articles/the-remarkable-chief-engineer/.
9. https://gibsonbiddle.medium.com/3-the-strategy-metric-tactic-lock-up-b7539ec69a7e.

Chapter 6
1. https://en.wikipedia.org/wiki/History_of_Linux#The_creation_of_Linux.
2. https://itsfoss.com/linux-runs-top-supercomputers/.
3. https://web.archive.org/web/20150806093859/http://www.w3cook.com/os/summary/.
4. https://project.linuxfoundation.org/hubfs/Reports/2021_LF_Annual_Report_010222
.pdf?hsLang=en.
5. https://bnoopy.typepad.com/bnoopy/2005/06/its_a_great_tim.html.
6. https://www.computerweekly.com/feature/Linuxworld-How-Amazon-saved-millions
-with-Linux.

7. https://twitter.com/danrose999/status/1347677573900242944.
8. Just for Fun: The Story of an Accidental Revolutionary.
9. http://www.catb.org/~esr/halloween/halloween1.html#quote8.
10. https://repo.or.cz/davej-history.git/blob/8bf26ec84e6362618e1abe641ac7f26c2674372 :/MAINTAINERS.
11. Torvalds described "good taste" in a TED interview as "seeing the big patterns and instinctively knowing what's the right way to do things." It is, for example, code without edge cases that gets the job done in the least complex way.
12. http://lkml.iu.edu/hypermail/linux/kernel/9809.3/0849.html.
13. http://lkml.iu.edu/hypermail/linux/kernel/9809.3/0957.html.
14. https://lwn.net/2002/0131/a/patch-penguin.php3.
15. https://lkml.org/lkml/2002/1/30/22.
16. https://en.wikipedia.org/wiki/BitKeeper.
17. BitKeeper had both technical and commercial limits. BitKeeper's "free users" license did not allow users to try copying it. But of course this was too tempting for the Linux community, and in 2005 the developer Andrew Trigdell began a project to reverse engineer BitKeeper, which led to the free-of-charge license to be revoked.
18. https://lore.kernel.org/lkml/CA+55aFy+Hv9O5citAawS+mVZO+ywCKd9NQ2wxUm Gsz9ZJzqgJQ@mail.gmail.com/.

Chapter 7

1. http://2012.conf.agile-france.org/conf.agile-france.org/index4ee5.html?speakers=le -secret-de-lamelioration-continue-atelier-piscar.
2. Marcus Buckingham and Ashley Goodall, *Nine Lies About Work*, Harvard Business Review Press, 2019, p. 33.
3. https://hbr.org/2020/11/how-apple-is-organized-for-innovation.
4. https://www.egonzehnder.com/insight/competencies-that-generate-growth-return-on -leadership.
5. https://rework.withgoogle.com/guides/managers-coach-managers-to-coach/steps/hold -effective-1-1-meetings/.
6. https://hbr.org/2019/03/the-future-of-leadership-development.
7. Robert C. Martin, *Clean Code*, Pearson Education, 2008, p. 66.
8. https://github.com/theodo/tyrion.
9. Martin Fowler, *Refactoring*, Addison-Wesley Signature Series, Pearson Education, 2008, p. 34.
10. https://www.lean.org/the-lean-post/articles/how-do-i-implement-5s-when-operators -think-everyone-does-things-a-little-differently/.

Chapter 8

1. Jim Gray, "A Conversation with Werner Vogels," *ACM Queue* 4, no. 4 (June 30, 2006), https://queue.acm.org/detail.cfm?id=1142065.
2. https://gist.Github.com/chitchcock/1281611.
3. https://www.gartner.com/en/newsroom/press-releases/2022-10-31-gartner-forecasts -worldwide-public-cloud-end-user-spending-to-reach-nearly-600-billion-in-2023.
4. https://en.wikipedia.org/wiki/EXtreme_Manufacturing.
5. https://medium.com/@mamblard75/the-software-defined-car-enabling-and-delivering -its-benefits-fb4bfc4f5666.
6. https://services.google.com/fh/files/misc/grab_n_go_white_paper.pdf.

Chapter 9

1. http://sunnyday.mit.edu/papers/therac.pdf.

Chapter 10

1. https://www.toyota-global.com/company/history_of_toyota/75years/text/taking_on_ the_automotive_business/chapter1/section1/item4.html.
2. "The moment a worker discovers a problem, he or she can summon the manager by pulling on a cord (the famous andon cord)," Jez Humble, Joanne Molesky, and Barry O'Reilly, *Lean Enterprise: How High Performance Organizations Innovate at Scale*, O'Reilly, 2015, p. 24.
3. https://engineering.fb.com/2017/08/31/web/rapid-release-at-massive-scale/.

Chapter 12

1. https://www.bbc.co.uk/news/science-environment-54979753.
2. https://dl.acm.org/doi/10.1109/ICSE.2017.75.
3. https://info.veracode.com/state-of-software-security-volume-11-flaw-frequency-by -language-infosheet-resource.html.
4. https://en.wikipedia.org/wiki/Type_system#Static_type_checking.
5. https://en.wikipedia.org/wiki/Void_safety.
6. https://www.infoq.com/presentations/Null-References-The-Billion-Dollar-Mistake-Tony -Hoare/.
7. https://www.typescriptlang.org/tsconfig#strictNullChecks.
8. https://www.figma.com/blog/inside-figma-a-case-study-on-strict-null-checks/.
9. https://www.gamedeveloper.com/programming/in-depth-functional-programming -in-c-.
10. https://en.wikipedia.org/wiki/Lint_%28software%2.
11. https://en.wikipedia.org/wiki/Test-driven_development.

Chapter 13

1. https://www.linkedin.com/pulse/la-plateforme-pour-300-milliards-d-de-pr%2525C3 %2525AAts-garantis-darves-bornoz%3FtrackingId=ggaFrSIHIl6zRgQCG8M0Tw %253D%253D/?trackingId=ggaFrSIHIl6zRgQCG8M0Tw%3D%3D.
2. https://www.tandfonline.com/doi/epdf/10.1080/00207547708943149?needAccess =true&role=button.

Chapter 14

1. https://www.tandfonline.com/doi/pdf/10.1080/00207547708943149.
2. https://www.amazon.co.uk/Kanban-Successful-Evolutionary-Technology-Business/ dp/0984521402.

Chapter 15

1. https://www.qagile.pl/wp-content/uploads/2017/01/Scrum-Guide-Feb-2010.pdf.
2. https://trunkbaseddevelopment.com/.
3. https://www.martinfowler.com/articles/branching-patterns.html.
4. https://www.infoq.com/news/2018/04/trunk-based-development/.
5. http://www.twisummit.cn/downloads/2007/Smalley_Origins_and_Facts_Regarding_ TPS.pdf.
6. https://spaceflight101.com/spx/spacex-raptor/.
7. https://aws.amazon.com/builders-library/going-faster-with-continuous-delivery/.

Chapter 16

1. https://engineering.fb.com/2017/08/31/web/rapid-release-at-massive-scale/.
2. https://www.lean.org/downloads/MITSloan.pdf.
3. https://www.wsj.com/articles/why-arent-there-enough-paper-towels-11598020793.

4. https://www.nationalgeographic.com/science/article/experts-warned-pandemic-decades-ago-why-not-ready-for-coronavirus.
5. https://www.theguardian.com/business/2021/mar/21/global-shortage-in-computer-chips-reaches-crisis-point.
6. https://www.reuters.com/article/us-japan-fukushima-anniversary-toyota-in-idUSKBN2B1005.
7. https://europe.autonews.com/automakers/toyota-breaks-profit-records-it-shrugs-pandemic-semiconductor-shortage.
8. https://www.just-auto.com/features/why-toyota-leads-the-global-automotive-sales-chart.

Chapter 17

1. https://www.fastcompany.com/1403230/googles-marissa-mayer-assaults-designers-data.
2. https://www.theguardian.com/technology/2014/feb/05/why-google-engineers-designers.
3. https://www.sec.gov/Archives/edgar/data/1018724/000119312514137753/d702518dex991.htm.
4. https://youtu.be/dxk8b9rSKOo?t=611.
5. https://cacm.acm.org/magazines/2016/7/204032-why-google-stores-billions-of-lines-of-code-in-a-single-repository/fulltext.
6. https://www.usenix.org/system/files/login/articles/login_1410_05_klein.pdf.
7. https://brandirectory.com/rankings/global/table.
8. https://ir.aboutamazon.com/news-release/news-release-details/2022/Amazon.com-Announces-Fourth-Quarter-Results/.
9. https://abc.xyz/investor/static/pdf/2022Q4_alphabet_earnings_release.pdf.
10. https://www.businessinsider.com/amazon-products-services-failed-discontinued-2019-3?r=US&IR=T#amazon-auction-25.
11. https://www.aboutamazon.com/news/company-news/2018-letter-to-shareholders.
12. The learning organization was popularised by David Garvin, professor at Harvard Business School and author of the most cited article on learning organizations, "Building a Learning Organization." According to Garvin, a learning organization is one that is "skilled at creating, acquiring, and transferring knowledge, and at modifying its behavior to reflect new knowledge and insights."

Chapter 18

1. https://www.amazon.jobs/en/principles.
2. https://ai.stanford.edu/~ronnyk/ExPThinkWeek2009Public.pdf.
3. https://hbr.org/2020/03/building-a-culture-of-experimentation.
4. The Innovator's Method, Harvard Business Review Press, 2014, p. 13.
5. https://hbr.org/2020/03/building-a-culture-of-experimentation.
6. Eric Ries, The Lean Startup: How Today's Entrepreneurs Use Continuous Innovation to Create Radically Successful Businesses, The Crown Publishing Group, 2011, p. 33.
7. Alexander Grosse and David Loftesness, Scaling Teams, O'Reilly Media, 2017.

Chapter 19

1. https://www.jstor.org/stable/2392547?seq=1#page_scan_tab_contents.
2. https://www.jstor.org/stable/2392547?seq=1#page_scan_tab_contents.
3. https://www.svpg.com/dedicated-product-teams/.
4. https://www.industryweek.com/leadership/companies-executives/article/21958928/training-within-industry-everything-old-is-new-again.
5. https://hbr.org/2006/03/connect-and-develop-inside-procter-gambles-new-model-for-innovation.
6. https://hbswk.hbs.edu/archive/pg-s-new-innovation-model.

7. Darius Mehri. *Notes from Toyota-land: An American Engineer in Japan*, Cornell University Press, 2005.
8. https://hbr.org/2004/09/perfecting-cross-pollination.

Chapter 20
1. https://hbr.org/2002/08/creativity-under-the-gun.
2. https://hbr.org/2019/11/why-constraints-are-good-for-innovation.
3. https://martinfowler.com/articles/developer-effectiveness.html.

Chapter 21
1. Marcus Buckingham and Ashley Goodall, *Nine Lies About Work*, Harvard Business Review Press, 2019, p. 53.
2. General Stanley McChrystal, David Silverman, Tantum Collins, and Chris Fussell, *Team of Teams*, Penguin Books, 2015, p. 216.
3. https://hbr.org/2014/12/the-google-way-of-attacking-problems.
4. https://en.wikipedia.org/wiki/Intelligence_cycle.
5. https://scholarsbank.uoregon.edu/xmlui/bitstream/handle/1794/11736/A%20brief%20introduction%20to%20CoP.pdf?sequence=1&isAllowed=y.
6. https://hbr.org/2000/01/communities-of-practice-the-organizational-frontier.
7. https://scholarsbank.uoregon.edu/xmlui/bitstream/handle/1794/11736/A%20brief%20introduction%20to%20CoP.pdf?sequence=1&isAllowed=y.
8. https://www.mckinsey.com/capabilities/mckinsey-digital/our-insights/fasttimes/interviews/beth-galetti.

ACKNOWLEDGMENTS

Many people have helped us with their knowledge, work, and time to create this book. We are incredibly grateful to all of you who contributed to our journey.

If we had to choose somewhere to start, it would be 2007, when we won the first prize of the Petit Poucet entrepreneurship contest. A massive thanks to Mathias Monribot, who gave us the impulse to become entrepreneurs by awarding us this prize and investing in us when we were only students. Thanks to Patrick Fleytoux, our expert accountant who has been at our side since the beginning, has helped us navigate the challenges of running a company, and through his wise advice has helped us avoid important mistakes. Thanks to our first investors Pierre Kosciusko-Morizet, Nicolas Bergerault, and François Bergerault, who trusted us way before it made sense for professional investors. And thanks to the Petit Poucet community of entrepreneurs that surrounded us and inspired us in those early years.

We wouldn't be where we are today without our clients, to whom we are immensely grateful for their trust and their challenges. A special mention to Pascal Loisel, the first one; Adrien and Romain Falcon, who helped us move forward when they challenged us to commit to Agile; Charles Berdugo, who trusted us on our first large-scale progressive migration; Laurent Kokanosky, the first leader in a large corporation to trust our Agile approach; Christian Dargnat, Pierre Moulin, Yohan Bayet, and Edouard Legrand, for launching and scaling together an entire Agile digital organization within a corporation; Bruno Delas for having the vision of Fast-IT, transforming alongside Victor Perez, Guilhem Grand, and many others a waterfall IT department to a state-of-the-art Agile organization deploying on demand; Arnaud Caudoux, Mathieu Heslouin, Sébastien Monchamps, and Nicolas Silberman for bringing us into their full-speed journey of supporting the French economy with digital; and all the other clients who have shaped us and trusted us along the years.

To all those who have joined our journey at one of the Theodo companies, we are incredibly thankful for your time, energy, and ingenuity contributing to develop and implement Theodo's ideas. Thanking you all individually here would add too many pages, but we hope the existence of this book makes up for it by helping spread the ideas that you have contributed to.

We are indebted to all the experts we met along the way in many different communities. The Symfony community with a special mention to Fabien Potencier, Thomas Rabaix, and François Baligant. The Agile community with a special mention to Christian Lapointe, Laurent Bossavit, Emmanuel Gaillot, Raphaël Pierquin, and Jonathan Perret. The devops community with a special mention to Patrick Debois, Jonathan Clarke, Brice Figureau, Arthur Gauthier, and Alexandre Rodière. Our incredible Lean Sensei, Antoine Contal, Régis Medina, and Michael Ballé, who have through their shared wisdom massively contributed to the content of this book. And the wider Lean community, with a special mention to Dan Jones, John Shook, Catherine Chabiron, and Sandrine Olivencia.

We were also helped by key partners to whom we are very thankful, a special mention to Lionel Touati, Matteo Pacca, Yassine Sekkat, Stéphane Bout, Philipp Hillenbrand, and Saumitra Ganguly.

We were lucky to meet some incredible coaches and mentors along the way, which we have to thank for helping us reframe our problems, in particular Xavier Weeger, Luc de Chammard, Sylvain Renault, and Hubert Raynier. This is also a role that our investors played, helping us see bigger—thank you, Philippe Crochet, Gérgoy Agez, Pierre Martini, Jean-François Rivassou, Jean-Marc Fiamma, and Matthieu Dordolo. The role is now officially taken on by the members of our advisory board— thank you, Camille Brégé, Pascal Delorme, François Hucher, and Pascal Imbert for the invaluable experience you bring.

We are not alone in exploring what Lean means in tech, and we are grateful to the founders and leaders we have been able to compare notes with—a special mention to Nicolas Chartier and Guillaume Paoli, Steve Anavi and Alexandre Prot, Sébastien Lucas, Jonathan Vidor, Jean-Baptiste Limare, Jérôme Lecat, Clément Ravouna, Sébastien Blanc, and the many members of the Galion think tank who have been invaluable sparring partners on the topic of scaling tech companies.

The ideas in this book would not exist without the many authors who inspired us. A special mention to Dan Jones and Jim Womack, Marty Cagan, General McChrystal, Colin Bryar and Bill Carr, Sadao Nomura, Gene Kim, Kevin Behr and George Spafford, Nicole Forsgren and Jez Humble, and Manuel Pais and Matthew Skelton.

Thank you very much, Catherine Chabiron, Régis Medina, and Antoine Haguenauer for writing the book *Learning to Scale at Theodo Group*. We are immensely grateful for your interest in our journey, and it has definitely prompted us to accelerate finishing our own book!

Finally, this book would not have come to fruition without some very key contributors. First, we have to thank Michael Ballé again, whose conversations in a bus in Japan gave us the initial spark. Thank you, Julie Berquez, for teaching us how to start a book. Thank you very much, Roberto Priolo, for having invested so much editing time and still showing enthusiasm every time. Thank you, Ingrid Case, for doing the final editing and supporting us during the critical home stretch of this project. And thank you, Casey Ebro and Christopher Brown, for making this book see the light.

INDEX

Page numbers followed by *f* and *t* refer to figures and tables, respectively.

ABOUT THE AUTHORS

Benoît Charles-Lavauzelle is the CEO and **Fabrice Bernhard** the CTO of Theodo, a leading technology consultancy they cofounded and scaled from $1 million in revenue and 10 people in 2012 to $100 million in revenue and 700 people in 2022. The company was featured in the "FT 1000: Europe's Fastest Growing Companies" and "Deloitte Technology Fast 500 EMEA" rankings and has been awarded the HappyIndex®AtWork label every year since 2015.

Based in New York, London, Paris, and Casablanca, Theodo uses Agile, devops, and Lean to build transformational tech products for clients all over the world, including global companies—such as VF Corporation, Raytheon Technologies, SMBC, Biogen, Colas, Tarkett, Dior, Safran, BNP Paribas, Allianz, and SG—and leading tech scale-ups—such as ContentSquare, ManoMano, and Qonto.

Benoît and Fabrice are experts in technology and large-scale transformations and have contributed to multiple startups scaling more sustainably with Lean thinking. They have been invited to share their experience at international conferences, including the Lean Summit, DevopsDays, and CraftConf. Their story has been featured in multiple articles and in the book *Learning to Scale at Theodo Group*.

Prior to Theodo, they had cofounded Allomatch.com, a digital platform for finding venues for where to watch sports, sold in 2019 to Fanzo.com, which had a combined audience of 6 million users in 2022.

Benoît is an active member of the Galion think tank and a prolific angel investor in tech, including success stories Aircall and Ubble. He studied at École Polytechnique and HEC and lives in Paris with his wife and three daughters.

Fabrice is the cofounder of the Paris Devops meetup and an active YPO member. He studied at École Polytechnique and ETH Zürich and lives in London with his two sons.